The Afterlife of Data

The Afterlife of Data

What Happens to Your Information When You Die and Why You Should Care

Carl Öhman

The University of Chicago Press ★ CHICAGO AND LONDON

The University of Chicago Press, Chicago 60637
The University of Chicago Press, Ltd., London

Published 2024
Printed in the United States of America

33 32 31 30 29 28 27 26 25 24   1 2 3 4 5

ISBN-13: 978-0-226-82822-0 (cloth)
ISBN-13: 978-0-226-82823-7 (e-book)
DOI: https://doi.org/10.7208/chicago/9780226828237.001.0001

Library of Congress Cataloging-in-Publication Data

Names: Öhman, Carl, author.
Title: The afterlife of data : what happens to your information when you die and why you should care / Carl Öhman.
Description: Chicago ; London : The University of Chicago Press, 2024. | Includes bibliographical references and index.
Identifiers: LCCN 2023026893 | ISBN 9780226828220 (cloth) | ISBN 9780226828237 (ebook)
Subjects: LCSH: Digital media—Social aspects. | Death—Social aspects. | Dead. | Future life. | Social media and society. | Digital preservation—Moral and ethical aspects.
Classification: LCC HM851 .O424 2024 | DDC 302.23/1—dc23/eng/20230620
LC record available at https://lccn.loc.gov/2023026893

♾ This paper meets the requirements of ANSI/NISO Z39.48-1992 (Permanence of Paper).

* For Marie

Contents

Introduction: A Collective Matter

> The dead make civilization.
> **Thomas Laqueur**

The New Natufians

One might imagine that in our nomadic origins, being human meant leaving things behind. Anything that could not be carried had to be abandoned—even people. When someone died, whether from old age, disease, or violence, they could not be brought along. Their bones were left to be slowly eaten by the earth. What could be carried on one's shoulders or dragged through the dirt had to serve the living; memories persisted only in the mind. This transitory life, shuffling from place to place, left little room for permanent memorialization. And so, without the material means to preserve the memory of those who had departed, a community would eventually forget the individuals inhabiting its past.

As this perpetual nomadic march of humanity finally ground to a halt, however, something had to change. With the establishment of the first permanent settlements, abandonment became impossible.[1] After all, if you are not walking away from the dead, they are certainly not walking away from you. Among the first known people to make this transition were the Natufians, a community living approximately where Israel is today. Like most cultures of the late Paleolithic, the

Natufians harvested wild grains and used stone tools. What distinguishes them in this setting is the emergence of a curious mortuary ritual, which would later become commonplace among Neolithic cultures. Rather than being left in the sand, the bodies of the dead would remain among the living, buried underneath their dwellings or in the walls connecting the homes of related families. More shocking, at least to us moderns, is that the head of the deceased would be removed, preserved, even decorated. Instead of flesh, plaster was added as a face; instead of eyes, seashells were placed in the empty sockets. The adorned skull would then be placed inside the clay dwellings of the living, alongside countless other skulls like it.[2] With time, the living Natufians would literally share their dwellings with the plaster faces of generations of ancestors staring back at them from the walls with glimmering seashell eyes.

This immediate proximity to the departed marked a major shift in history. To paraphrase Robert Pogue Harrison, it provided a platform where two worlds, one above ground and another beneath, could come to interpret one another.[3] It reinforced the sense that the dead remained present in the affairs of the living, which, some say, laid the very foundation for human civilization. And indeed, over the millennia that have elapsed since the Neolithic, new, less morbid versions of the same head removal custom kept emerging. Roman aristocratic funerals, for instance, would sometimes feature painted, so-called *imago* masks, made from wax imprints of deceased ancestors' faces and worn by actors to symbolize the welcoming of the newly departed into the ancestral community. In ancient Egypt, the bodies of the dead were famously embalmed in their entirety, buried under some of the greatest architectonic wonders our species has ever seen.

In a sense, we still live in the worlds of the dead insofar as we continue to speak their languages, to inhabit their cities and lands, and to build on their legacies. In short, wherever there have been humans, their culture has been informed by the ways they have dealt with past members of their community. As historian Thomas Laqueur concisely put it, "The dead make civilization."[4]

Despite these updated ways of keeping the dead (symbolically) present within the domestic environment, the long-term historical trend has been their gradual removal from our daily living spaces. In modernity—the era referred to by scholars as the age of "forbidden death"—the dead have little to no presence.[5] They are seen as a disruption of the order of things, a disturbance that must be concealed at any cost. Few moderns (at least among younger generations) have ever even seen a dead body, let alone witnessed someone's death. Instead, the departed members of modern communities have been exiled to places where we do not need to think about them, except perhaps on given occasions like All Hallows' Eve or an occasional funeral. They are hidden from everyday life, confined to cemeteries and archives, which are technically open to visitors but could ultimately be left and forgotten at will. In modernity, the dead have tended to be *elsewhere*.

Until now. Today, they are again entering our dwellings, except that those dwellings tend to be online platforms rather than clay houses. Instead of craniums in walls, the faces of the dead stare back at us through the social media profiles they leave behind, through the photo libraries we keep in our smartphones, and through the myriad traces people leave behind in their daily online activities. They remain perpetually present, and increasingly numerous by the day—so numerous, in fact, that on several social networks they may come to outnumber living users' profiles within only a few decades. So, if the dead "make civilization," our civilization seems to stand before a shift on par with that of the first Paleolithic settlers. We are the new Natufians.

What Do We Do with the Digital Dead?

In the age of digital media, recording has become the default mode of society. Nearly everything we do leaves some kind of trace behind, whether we intend it or not. Our behavioral and social patterns are recorded by the social media platforms we use to communicate, our taste in music and film is stored by the streaming services we use for entertainment, our consumer patterns are logged by our credit cards, and our search data are recorded and stored on one of Google's roughly 2.5 million servers.[6] Even "offline" activities end up on servers. Many apps send geolocation signals every two seconds, giving an almost perfect record of their users' whereabouts. The Apple Health app, for example, which comes preinstalled on every iPhone, automatically tracks every step a user takes and logs it in the cloud. So, in case you are an Apple user, there's a file of data somewhere giving a pretty accurate picture of how fit (or unfit) you have been over the years. Regardless of whether you use the internet actively or not, your life produces an ever-swelling volume of data—a digital shadow that grows increasingly similar to you.

In their totality, these data become an almost perfect imprint—a hyperrealistic and three-dimensional *imago* mask, printed not in wax but in ones and zeros. Yet unlike our biological bodies, and unlike wax, this new digital imprint will not deteriorate after your death. Unless corrupted or intentionally deleted, it will remain intact, untouched by the inevitable fate of all organic life. When we encounter the dead through their left-behind data—what researchers call "digital remains"—we are not merely facing a symbolic mask but a lifetime of data, an informational corpse.[7]

Meanwhile, the technological means to process and "mine" our data is developing at breakneck speed. In the name of targeted advertisement, an entire industry has grown to predict people's behavior based on their data trails. The most famous example, perhaps, is how Target used a teenage girl's credit card records to predict that she was pregnant before her parents had found out.[8] It is not a perfect example, since, after all, there are some things that only pregnant women will buy. But targeted ads, boosted by the fast development of artificial intelligence (AI), have come a long way. Provided sufficient data, today's algorithms may even be able predict your pregnancy before you know it yourself. In fact, they work so well that many people are convinced that their phones "listen" to their conversations to suggest ads for products they have mentioned. The truth is that the heaps of data that people leave behind, combined with the razorlike sharpness of AI, make people much more predictable than their imaginations allow them to comprehend. If you do not believe me, just log into OpenAI's ChatGPT, give it some text you have written, and ask it to reproduce a new text in the same style. If it looks just like the kind of thing you would have written, do not despair; most people are that predictable, and so are the texts they write.

Predictive algorithms do not care whether a person is alive or dead. With enough data they can be trained to predict what someone *would* do, say, or sound like, were they still alive. Amazon recently announced a new feature for their voice assistant Alexa, which, when fed as little as one minute of recorded audio, lets the assistant speak in the voice of a deceased relative. Similarly, a project in the Netherlands set out to produce a "new" Rembrandt painting, based on all available data on his work. An AI application analyzed every possible aspect of Rembrandt's style—lighting, motif, brush strokes, angles, and so on—and from those patterns emerged what to most people would appear to be an authentic Rembrandt portrait. The same has been done to complete Beethoven's unfinished Tenth Symphony. In fact, the app Historical Figures even lets users "chat" with dead historical figures, including Adolf Hitler and Jesus of Nazareth, based on what is historically known about them. With relatively small amounts of data, AI can turn anyone's legacy into an interactive agent.

Naturally, even the most modest internet user leaves much more information about themselves than Rembrandt or Beethoven did. And just as Rembrandt's paintings reveal a pattern that can be replicated, so do our digital remains, only our patterns are a lot more detailed. Your personality can literally be extracted from the data you leave behind. As this book will cover in detail, there is even a budding industry around it. MIT start-up Eterni.me, for example, offers users a virtual avatar which, based on their data profile, talks, looks, and behaves just like them.[9] The idea is that this artificial agent will make users "virtually immortal" and allow them to chat with their descendants. A new competitor, Hereafter AI, offers the same product, and Microsoft recently filed a patent for a similar product. Soon, our online social presence may no longer be limited to static photos and records of information but will become an interactive agent that responds to new input, or at least continues to produce new content. The faces staring back from the walls of our digital dwellings, in other words, are beginning to speak with voices of their own.

This may sound more like science fiction than real life. Yet, the automation of our online afterlife presence is not some distant futuristic dream. Nor is it necessarily very high-tech. On the contrary, it is an increasingly widespread phenomenon, running mostly on mobile devices, which is often paired with religious and cultural customs around the world. Consider the increasingly popular phenomenon of Islamic prayer apps. These nascent services automatically send out supplications (a form of Islamic prayer) from their subscribers' social media profiles—subscribe and the app will take care of your religious online presence for you—often with the explicit promise to continue posting after their users' deaths.[10] As I will show later in this book, these apps generate millions of automated tweets every day, tweets that are increasingly posted from the dead. This is to say that, contrary to common belief, the most common form of automated posthumous presence is not due to some sophisticated Silicon Valley start-up but arises from the ancient and spiritual practice of prayer. Moreover, such tweets do not necessarily present themselves explicitly as coming from the afterlife, since the profiles from which the content is posted remain intact. You have likely already encountered online content posted by deceased users—you just do not know it yet.

The most fundamental shift, however, is not the new interactivity of the dead, but their constant *accessibility*. Most of us now have one or several departed friends whose faces continue popping up in our feeds, or whose photos and old messaging logs we return to for comfort. Unlike a grave or a physical photo album, digital remains are accessible from virtually anywhere, with an unprecedented level of granularity. My own grandfather, for instance, who passed away a few years ago, remains constantly within my reach. Whenever I want to, I can pick up my phone, open the Instagram app, and watch a video of him skiing in the Swedish mountains. I can hear his jolly voice, read our conversations, and laugh at his ironic comments on my agitated political posts. I can even post something on his Facebook timeline. A part of him remains *there*, and the same goes for nearly every person I know who has died. In the ether, they are still present, constantly on call in one's pocket, alongside all the others you know and regularly communicate with. Wherever you go, the dead go with you.

Like the emergence of the first permanent settlements in the late Paleolithic, this constant presence of the dead marks a major shift in how we relate to our past and the individuals who inhabit it. It introduces a new mode of being with the dead, which I shall refer to as a *post-mortal condition* throughout this book. By "post-mortal" I am certainly not referring to some form of digital immortality, by which our souls live on in electronic format. Such a prospect has become a fantasy among so-called transhumanist communities, who believe that the digital revolution is the next step in human evolution, but it has little to do with reality, at least for the foreseeable future (and then some).[11] I am also not saying that our digital remains will necessarily endure in perpetuity. Digital data are, like everything else in the world, dependent on material objects for their existence—wires, servers, networks, and so on.[12] Like everything else surrounding us, their longevity is subject to the laws of thermodynamics. We are, and will always remain, fundamentally finite. What the post-mortal condition denotes is rather a reconfiguration of the relationship between the living and the dead, a mode of being whereby the dead remain present among the living by default. Unlike previous technologies used to preserve the dead—cemeteries, archives, photo albums—the internet is no longer something that we visit and leave. It is something that we live *inside*. Today, no one says that they are "going online" or that they are "offline" whenever they do not use the internet. We are constantly connected, constantly *within* the network. Even if you do not have your phone or laptop with you, you may be close to a car, a fridge, or a TV that is connected to the internet. According to a white paper by Juniper Research, the total number of connected devices is expected to reach eighty-three billion by 2024.[13] In this giant network of connected devices, we live *onlife*, to use a term coined by philosopher Luciano Floridi, in a mode of being where everything is always at hand—even the past.[14] For the first time in thousands of years, we live within the same matrix as the dead through the connected archives of the web. The border that once separated our world from theirs is rapidly eroding.

I describe our new co-dwelling with the dead as a *condition* because it remains an open question how, if at all, we as a society choose to live with the presence of the past generation. To be sure, this is not a retreat to some original, more natural relationship to them. As philosopher Hans Ruin reminds us, "the ethical and political interaction between the dead and the living will always remain an open challenge, not just a case of being either with or without the dead."[15] I could not agree more, but the point here is that this open challenge is never neutrally manifested to us. It manifests itself in the technological and material circumstances under which the dead remain present. As such, the advent of the internet, and the emergence of the *onlife* mode of being, changes the conditions under which we interact with, interpret, and negotiate with the dead. Just like the Natufians were suddenly faced with the question of what to do with the bodies of the dead, we too are now faced with the question of how to deal with their digital presence. They are *there*, and they will not go away unless we actively remove them.

Everyone's Concern

This book sheds light on the ethical, political, and economic challenges that arise from our post-mortal condition. This is something that affects us all. As we know from personal experience, dealing with the posthumous presence of the deceased can be a difficult process for someone who has just lost a loved one, especially for the next of kin. If the departed person leaves no passwords behind, how does one take down their online accounts and profiles? How does one notify online contacts of their death? And what about their digital assets, subscriptions, and virtual avatars? These are questions that people do not normally walk around thinking about. They pose new and often intimidating challenges, ones for which we have little or no preparation. Moreover, online platforms are rarely designed with such questions in mind, meaning that interfaces can be less than accommodating when one tries to remove a profile or report a user as deceased—especially for an elderly person unfamiliar with apps and websites. On top of this, the presence of a deceased person's digital remains also raises questions of a more ethical nature. Should the online presence of a person be deleted upon death? Or, on the contrary, is it imperative to preserve it? Who has the authority to decide? Does a dead person still have a right to privacy? And what about the companies that own and control their data—what should their responsibility be? Answering these questions is a responsibility that ultimately falls on each of us as individuals.

At the same time, we are also facing such questions collectively, as a society, or better, as a civilization, responding to the lingering presence of past generations. Here, our individual experiences are secondary, for we are each affected, whether we or our loved ones use the internet or not. According to the United Nations' population projections, around 2.2 billion people are expected to pass away within the next three decades alone (almost eight billion over the course of the century), many leaving a considerable volume of data behind.[16] These data will eventually fill up the servers of the platforms we use for daily communication. As I outline in some detail in chapter 2, the dead on Facebook may even come to outnumber the living as soon as 2070. If the network continues to grow at current rates, it will have accumulated close to five billion profiles of deceased users—from virtually all around the world—by the end of the century. Every social network, every business that gathers data about its consumers is facing a similar future. At some point the users or consumers will die. Then what? For Facebook, allowing bereaved families either to remove the profile or to turn it into a digital memorial has served as a temporary solution. But what happens as the custodians of the memorials also pass away? And as the servers are slowly taken over by the dead, which threatens the very business model of ad-driven platforms, the question remains: What do you do with their data? What *should* be done with their data?

As I will stress repeatedly throughout this book, whatever the answer is, the implications go far beyond the consequences for individual users. Insofar as the dead "make civilization," this is a concern for entire societies, not just individuals and their families. Why? Because the digital remains of the billions of individuals who use the internet today amount to something more than a collection of individual user histories. In aggregate, they also constitute our *collective* digital past—the basis for our society's relationship to its former members. Arguably, the flood of data we produce today constitutes the biggest archive of human behavior in the history of our species. It may even become the primary source of historical information that we pass down to future generations—humanity's shared digital cultural heritage.[17] We ought to be careful about how we manage it.

Unlike previous forms of historical resources, our aggregated digital remains are not only a reflection or representation of life in the early twenty-first century—increasingly, they *are* life in the twenty-first century. In the onlife world, the dichotomy between on- and offline becomes trivial because our lives together increasingly take place *within* the network. Events and movements such as Black Lives Matter, #MeToo, and the Arab Spring uprisings are, to a large extent, born digital. Their data traces are not merely representations of events taking place "in real life." They have had an online existence from the very beginning. As such, they will become an invaluable source of information to future generations seeking to understand their past. Imagine, for a second, if we had access to Napoleon Bonaparte's Facebook messages, or the data patterns of the German population in the 1930s. The lessons learned would be endless.

Some may consider what we post on social media to be no more than "trash." But trash is in fact among the richest sources of information about ancient cultures. Temples and monuments may tell us much about the elites that governed ancient civilizations, yet they disclose little about the everyday lives of the ordinary people who lived under them. What people consider mundane, by contrast, is often rich with information about their daily lives. Moreover, due to the ubiquity of the internet and its worldwide reach, we have, maybe for the first time ever, an opportunity to create a historical record that genuinely reflects the diversity of human life, not just the select (male) elite that has dominated the records left to us by our forebears. As such, the accumulation of digital remains raises questions that have not occurred to any previous generation, questions of what we owe to the past generations who linger on our servers, and to future ones, who will depend on these same records to understand their past. Who owns and has authority to control these data? What principles should guide their preservation? And how should it all be governed? As will become clear throughout this book, there is a considerable discrepancy between how we *should* answer these questions and how our digital remains are currently managed.

Back in 2002, historian Roy Rosenzweig noted that "our most important and imaginatively construed digital collections are in private hands," which, he warned, would pose "grave dangers to the future of the past."[18] The two decades that have passed since have not proved him wrong. Digital data are increasingly concentrated around a handful of powerful private actors, which has led to power asymmetries of unprecedented proportions. Never before have so few had so much control over so much information about the past, and with it, the power to shape the present. And the imbalance is only growing. As I discuss in chapter 4, this poses a grave political threat. George Orwell warned in *Nineteen Eighty-Four* that "who controls the past controls the future."[19] In a couple of decades, it may not be Orwell's evil party that controls the past but a single for-profit corporation. If Meta (Facebook), Google, and a handful of actors like them continue to monopolize our digital past, it is not inconceivable that they would use this power, intentionally or unintentionally, to advance their political and economic interests.

The corporate control of our digital heritage is also problematic in relation to the selection of what materials are worth preserving. Contrary to what people often expect, digital data are fragile, and they are often corrupted or destroyed if not properly managed. "Digital information lasts forever—or five years, whichever comes first," as phrased by digital preservationist Jeff Rothenberg.[20] Archives require constant care to remain useful and readable—file formats must be changed, hardware needs to be replaced, and systems need to be updated and organized. All of which are labor-intensive undertakings. In the face of limited resources, some data—or some*one's* data—need to be weeded out. And this requires some form of criteria for which data have "worth," some principle that helps guide the selection process. Unfortunately, the present system does not permit us to collectively ask ourselves what these principles should be, because today, our digital remains—the fabric of our collective digital past—are predominantly owned and controlled by private for-profit corporations. And for a for-profit enterprise, only one type of value counts: profit. If you do not keep up with the capital accumulation of your competitors, you are doomed to fail. It does not matter how much nonmonetary value (e.g., beauty, happiness, honor) a company generates—if it does not lead to long-term economic growth, it is doomed. In sum, if we leave the management of our collective digital past solely in the hands of the industry, the question "What should we do with the data of the dead?" becomes solely a matter of "What parts of the past can we make money on?" We replace the open discussion on what principles should guide the selection of resources passed down to future generations with a system that can only appreciate one value: capital.

The stakes involved in the fate of our digital remains could hardly be higher. Humanity is at the risk of losing access to its collective past and ending up in what archivists call a "digital dark age."[21] Or worse, we may end up with a hugely asymmetrical distribution of power over the data that remain. Even if you do not plan on dying anytime soon, and even if you may not personally care about what anyone does to your data after your death, the future of the past is, or should be, the concern of *everyone*. This book shows why and how.

* * *

What I have emphasized so far is that our relationship with the dead is experiencing a fundamental shift. What is at stake is not just posthumous privacy, or our ability to visit some deceased relative's Facebook profile, but our civilization's very relationship to its future past. In our new mode of being with the dead, the post-mortal condition, the past and its dead have once again become present to us. And this presence forces us to ask new difficult questions: How should we organize the management of digital remains? How can we gain more control over our collective digital legacy? What do we owe to future generations? And whose responsibility is it?

These are big ethical questions without any obvious answers. The goal of this book is not to provide a clear-cut solution or blueprint for how to solve them. In fact, part of my argument is that they cannot be solved by one person, for they require *democratic deliberation*. As with all matters of political significance, there is no objectively superior solution, independent of what goals we consider worth pursuing. Whatever road we settle upon will be full of conflicts between the many stakeholders involved. Toward the end of the book, however, I shall offer some sense of direction to guide us forward as we moderate these conflicts. For one thing is certain: whatever road we settle upon, we must walk it together. The living, the dead, and the unborn all have a stake in how we steward our synthetic environment. We hold this responsibility not only as social media users and mourning individuals, but as *archeopolitans*—citizens of an archive inhabited by the ongoing project we call humanity. Like the Paleolithic tribes before us, we must learn how to live with a new kind of presence of the dead, to be good archeopolitans. This could mean actively removing the dead from our servers, but then we must ask whom to remove first, and what to do when we disagree on the answer. It also could mean finding ways of making the dead part of everyday life again, but then we need to agree on how, and who should carry the cost, not least in terms of the carbon footprint of data storage. It could also mean everything in between these extremes. The point is that we have to choose. Indeed, the emergence of the post-mortal condition is a radical reconfiguration of society's relationship with its past members, but it is not a mechanical process. It is and will always remain an *open* challenge.

1 * From Bones to Bytes

> As homo sapiens we are born out of our biological parents.
> As humans we are born of the dead.
>
> **Robert Pogue Harrison**

> To be ignorant of what occurred before you were born is to remain always a child. For what is the worth of human life, unless it is woven into the life of our ancestors by the records of history?
>
> **Cicero**

Beginnings

Those who do not know their history remain children. For a child, everything is for the first time, the world a mysterious and unpredictable place. It is only when relating events to the past, both one's own and that of one's surroundings, that the events around us begin to mean something. The unknown beings of the world outside the womb become parents, siblings, friends, or enemies only in reference to their *past* actions. It is by relating today to yesterday that we anticipate tomorrow, and only by anticipation can we make meaning and take command.

Something similar can be said about communities undergoing radical change. A community without a past is a community that has lost control of itself. If we do not know from which port we departed, we cannot know our direction even if our location is known, and so it becomes hopeless to take command of the ship that is society. For any study of society's future—and this book is above all a study of the future—we must therefore begin by turning our gaze backward to locate our point of departure. For the purposes of this book, this means that our first question ought to be: How have we lived with the dead in the past? Only in light of this question can we begin assessing how the digital revolution is reconfiguring our relationship to the dead, and what that process ought to look like.

I realize the gargantuan proportions of this question. Since the presence of the dead constitutes a cornerstone in just about every human institution—from religion to language to architecture—it is impossible to account for changes in the social role of the dead without also telling the entire story of our kind. Such a scope is far beyond what any single chapter, or even book, can hope to accomplish. Instead, let us focus on a more specific question, namely: What can we learn from previous technological disruptions of our relationship with the dead?[1] The response that I lay out in the following pages is threefold: (1) From the emergence of the first permanent settlements, when the dead became inescapably present among the living, we learn that the technological mediation of the dead is what makes civilization possible, that humans always live within a world built by the dead. (2) From the invention of written language, we learn that the advent of the digital is merely the latest chapter in a quest as old as humanity, a quest to decouple dead persons from their corporeal presence by providing a portable prosthetic voice, face, or body of information that can travel far beyond biological confines. (3) And finally, from the triumph of the cremation furnace in the nineteenth century, we learn about the cultural backdrop against which the current disruption is taking place: the hidden death of modernity.

These three lessons do not necessarily align to a linear narrative. History rarely does. Still, we need to begin at the very beginning, in what the historian Thomas Laqueur calls *the deep time of the dead*, when the presence of the departed consisted of little more than a collection of bones.[2]

The Deep Time of the Dead

According to the German philosopher Hans-George Gadamer, caring for the dead is an exclusively human endeavor, a "conduct of life that has spiralled out of the order of nature."[3] In this view, animals have no concept of a personhood beyond physical presence and hence show little interest in their deceased kin. Caring for the absent, and specifically the ritual of burial, is thus what sets us apart from other organisms on this earth. Recent ethological research, however, casts serious doubt on these speculations, at least if we are to read them literally. Many animals—including wolves, chimpanzees, elephants, dolphins, otters, geese, sea lions, and magpies (yes, really!)—do in fact mourn their dead, sometimes for days.[4] Elephants have even been observed standing by the carcasses of their dead offspring for *weeks*, and they often take great interest in skeletal remains of their kin, as well as those of individuals unrelated to their herd. (Some observations suggest elephants' attempts at burying, or at least covering the remains of, other elephants with leaves and sand.) In other words, caring for and relating to the dead has not spiraled "out of" nature but is one of our deepest instincts, shared with many other members of the animal kingdom.

Still, we should not judge Gadamer too quickly. After an animal's corporeal body has decomposed, the sole expression of its presence is a pile of bones, and (if it has been lucky) the genetic code passed down to its offspring. The animal successor will eventually find itself in nothing more than a habitat, a surrounding of mere practical utility. Humans, on the other hand, do not live only in habitats, but always within the *worlds* inherited from those who came before. We do not inherit merely our ancestors' DNA, but also their language, culture, and ideologies, as well as the physical infrastructures they built to keep society afloat. We do not live only through the genetic information of our forebears, but through and within the cultural information they left behind for us. In fact, imagining a human that does not live in such a world is impossible, for a creature that did not live in a world created by humans, or something like humans, would not be part of the intergenerational project we know as *humanity*.

No one has framed this more eloquently than Stanford literary scholar Robert Pogue Harrison in his claim "As *Homo sapiens* we are born of our biological parents. As human beings we are born of the dead."[5] Indeed, to be a member of humanity requires more than a mere biological qualification. To be human is, above all, to "come after those who came before," to borrow another one of Harrison's phrases.[6] In any case, human beings are, and have always been, in constant correspondence with their past. We live in and through a constant relationship to those who came before. The very fact that you can read these letters is a heritage from the Roman Empire, whose alphabet we inherited; it is a heritage from the Anglo-Saxons, in whose language we are now communicating. The fact that these words have any meaning whatsoever is only because they point backward in time, not to some original point of reference, but to an endless sequence of references that reaches all the way back to the animal kingdom and beyond. "Humanity begins where there is already an ancestor,"[7] to borrow one last phrase from Harrison.

Yet our story needs to commence somewhere, and for this book, I would like to place that "somewhere" at the eclipse of the Paleolithic, right at the erection of the first permanent settlements. For the Paleolithic nomad, the presence of past generations was limited. Being human, as it were, was to leave things behind—including people. Although tribes probably returned to the same areas on yearly basis, they were not permanently attached. Life was to travel onward in small hunter-gatherer bands, following the change of seasons and the migration of game. Archaeological evidence from this time period is sparse. We cannot know exactly how prehistoric humans dealt with, and related to, their deceased kin. But insofar as today's surviving nomadic cultures give any clues (a deterministic assumption, to be sure), the dead were probably not a very active part of social life, at least not as distinguishable individuals. Contemporary nomadic tribes, like Bedouins, put little effort into burial.[8] Bodies are generally covered with an anonymous heap of sand or stone and then abandoned. Only rarely are the dead spoken of thereafter.[9] This custom has stayed roughly the same for hundreds, perhaps thousands, of years. Given the practical conditions of a nomadic lifestyle, it was probably once shared by all of humanity.

Of course, the dead may live on through legends, songs, and traditions and as part of an imagined greater spirit that inhabits the land. Yet, while such biological memory is easy to carry, it is also fickle, deceptively plastic, and it puts a definitive cap on the number of individuals who can be remembered by a community—a weak guarantee for a continuing social presence. Unless the dead are symbolically transferred to an external object like wood, stone, or clay, a tribe simply cannot carry the dead around with them. Hence, to survive over time, especially to transcend generations, the memory of the departed needs a mark, a physical structure on which the permanence of the dead can be projected. It needs some form of inscription in the landscape.[10]

It should not be surprising, therefore, that the first human-made permanent structures were allegedly erected not to seek shelter or store food but to preserve the memory of past members of the community. At first, these constructions were probably not much more than a heap of stones, or a mound of dirt and sand, something that provided a tangible surface onto which the memory of the dead could be projected. But with time they developed into proper sepulchres, or at least constructions with an interior, a secluded space within which the dead could dwell. This is what Spanish philosopher Miguel de Unamuno meant by his famous observation that "stone was used for sepulchres before it was used for houses."[11] The American historian Lewis Mumford speculates along the same lines, in his classic book *The City in History*, noting that "the dead were the first to have a permanent dwelling."[12] These initial stone monuments, claims Mumford, were landmarks to which the living probably returned at intervals, "to commune with or placate the ancestral spirits."[13] That is to say, the areas where the dead were laid to rest became given points of reference in the natural landscape.

The idea that the dead were the first to have permanent dwellings is not only historically accurate, it also holds a deeper truth. For a sepulchre is in fact a sort of house—a house for the dead. Or perhaps we should say that a house is a kind of grave for the living. Archaeologists hypothesize that when the first permanent settlements emerged at the dawn of the Neolithic, the burial sites of the dead were the first to be populated, due to their already established status as meeting places. The living were newcomers here. They moved into a domain originally reserved for the inhabitants of the past, with whom they now had to share their dwellings—often literarily. The Natufians, by reference to whom I opened this book, are an illustrative case. This was a culture that emerged around the Levant (i.e., the area of present-day Palestine, Israel, Jordan, and Syria). Apart from their being among the first cultures known to brew beer (!), Natufian society was a lot like one would imagine. They harvested grains, used stone tools, and had an early form of class society. What makes them interesting in this context, however, is their mortuary rituals. Whereas their Paleolithic predecessors had merely left the dead in the sand and walked away, this custom became impossible for the settled Natufians. And as such, they were faced with the inevitable question of how to dispose of their ancestors' bodies. The answer was to keep them underneath the very houses in which they lived. And not only that—before this "disposal" of the body, the head of the deceased would first be severed and adorned with a plaster face and seashell eyes. These decorated craniums were then placed within the dwellings to remain within the world of the living. As vividly described by the leading burial archaeologist Mike Parker Pearson:

> While corpses lay buried directly beneath the feet of the living, their skulls continued to share the surface world of the living until they were deposited in caches within pits, on

> house floors, or other contexts. Both corpse and skull, however, shares the spatial locale of the living. Such was people's concern with the maintaining this thread of place and space that generations on generations lived in the same place, building their mudbrick houses on top of previous dwellings until the surface of their inhabitation, human-made hills of mud known as *tells*, towered above the surrounding plain.[14]

The world of the living and the world of the dead were, in other words, one. This new and permanent proximity to the dead marked a radical shift in the nature of their presence. They had become just as much a part of society, just as permanent, as the houses under which they lay buried, their gaze as open as the seashells that glimmered from the walls. As historian William Spellman puts it, this presence "reinforced the conviction that they [the dead] remained involved in current affairs."[15] And insofar as people thought the dead remained involved in the affairs of the living, they actually *were*, albeit perhaps no longer as sentient agents. They had lost the ability to speak, yet their prosthetic eyes provided a new surface for projection.

Although most cultures have not removed and decorated the skulls of their deceased kin, many subsequent mnemonic rituals have a kinship with those observed among the Natufians. The human-shaped clay figures found by archaeologists all over Europe and the Near East are one example. Although they were once believed to be statues of fertility goddesses, there is now a great deal of evidence to suggest that these figures are in fact symbolic incarnations of ancestors. They are, for instance, often found in caches alongside skulls. Their facial features resemble those of the plaster faces of the Natufian skulls (great detail in every feature except the mouth, including seashell eyes, etc.), and they are often found at similar locations within the dwellings of the living: inside walls or in joins between houses (supposedly signifying links between families related to a common ancestor). According to Parker Pearson, these statues represent a "transformation from the representation of ancestors in a literal sense, using the actual skull, to a more figurine sense, portraying the deceased individual separately from their physical elements."[16] Later these representations would develop into yet more abstract forms, such as anthropomorphized pots, or, in Hellenic and Roman culture, death masks known as *imago masks*, facial imprints in wax reserved for highly distinguished (male) citizens. These masks were used mainly to represent the dead during funerals of prominent individuals, where they would be worn by actors whose physical constitutions resembled the originals. Seated at ivory chairs facing the living, the actor wearing the imago mask would make the dead "come alive," or at least give a convincing visual impression that they were actually present. The ritual symbolized the dead welcoming the newly deceased to their community but also tied generations together under a single roof. Just as the Natufian skulls were placed within the joins of houses, so the imago masks became the joins of the empire. It showed that Rome endured, and it cemented the patria, the fatherland, as the permanent inhabitancy—the *house*, as it were—of multiple generations.

Still to this day, houses remain symbols of the union between the living and the dead. Indeed, few tropes invoke such ghostly connotations as abandoned houses, with their past inhabitants somehow still lingering. There is also an obvious lexical connection in that the English word *house*, which most commonly refers to a physical structure, may just as well refer to a lineage, a community of dead and alive members. Perhaps, one always implies the existence of the other—there is no such thing as a home without a past, and no such thing as a past without a house where it can reside. The idea that the house shared by present and past generations constitutes the origin of human civilization is perhaps more dramaturgical convenience than historical fact. Yet, there is no doubt that the effects of the proximity to the dead, afforded by the first houses, have reverberated through the centuries. If nothing else, the house has remained one of the most powerful metaphors for what it means to be with (or *within*) one's past, and thereby what it means to be human. This much we should grant Gadamer.

The Portable Dead

Among the literary artifacts to reach us from the depths of history, none are older than the story known as the *Epic of Gilgamesh*.[17] The epic begins by outlining the adventures and friendship of the hero, Gilgamesh, King of Uruk, and his friend Enkidu. After Gilgamesh and Enkidu slay both the monster Humbaba and the beast known as the Bull of Heaven, the gods decide that enough is enough. As punishment for the hubris of the two companions, the gods have Enkidu killed by infecting him with a disease that plagues him for twelve days (not a hero's death, exactly). This brings Gilgamesh to a painful awareness of his own finitude. He sets out on yet another heroic quest—to cheat death once and for all, achieving immortality. His search eventually leads him to a man named Utnapishtim, who, along with his wife, is one of the only two individuals ever granted eternal life by the gods. Utnapishtim tries to convince Gilgamesh to accept the inevitability of his fate, but he eventually yields and reveals the location of a magic herb growing on the seafloor, which Gilgamesh may use to gain immortality. Gilgamesh actually finds and harvests the plant at the given location, but on his journey homeward, it is snatched by a snake while Gilgamesh is off swimming. Alas, he has to return to Uruk empty-handed. Ironically, though, this very failure has made Gilgamesh one of the immortal figures of literature. The memory of the king who sought infinity—who some claim is based on a real person—remains present in our collective consciousness to this day. His story prevails in the myriad of subsequent epics that it has inspired over the millennia, and also in the literal sense that it is itself one of the most famous pieces of literature of all time, a key reading at any literature studies program around the globe. This everlasting status owes thanks to a power much stronger than any magic herb: the power of the written word.

Writing has much in common with the construction of houses and graves, so much that we may even consider the written word a continuation, or extension, of the house. If, as I have suggested, we think of houses and mounds as *inscriptions in the landscape*, then the letter is nothing more than a sepulchre on the miniature landscape of a sheet of paper, a clay tablet, or a computer monitor. Or vice versa: graves are a form of writing in soil. In many languages, words relating to writing (such as the English *engraving*, French *engraver*, Proto-Slavic *_gretì_, and so on) and words for "grave" share the same etymological root, the Proto-Indo-European word *$g^{h}reb^{h}$-. Writing a letter, then, is analogue to digging a grave on a paper. And on an empirical level, writing was once intimately associated with burial. In ancient Egypt, for example, officials often had their biographies inscribed on their tombs long before their deaths. It was a key part of both the embalming process and the construction of the grave chamber itself.[18] The ancient Egyptians would even leave letters for the dead when visiting their graves. The dead were apparently not able to hear the oral messages of the living, but when words were inscribed on papyrus, it seems they were considered able to transcend whatever boundaries separated the two worlds. As explained by Ruin, the grave was a "formative analogy to the book, there the text makes present a subject that belongs to the world of the dead."[19] The written word, like the grave, is a kind of container wherein the dead reside and remain fixed over time, thereby gaining a prosthetic voice independent of the living. Both the word and the grave are containers of time, material interfaces where the present and the past come to meet.

Like houses and graves, the written word is something that humans reside *within*. It is the cultural fabric that encloses us from nature. Like the stone sepulchre, it *contains* the dead. Because, as we have seen, being human is to always reside in a world, and worlds always consist of languages forged across generations.[20] The written word, that is, is a portable dwelling of the dead. Portability, in this context, means two things. On the one hand, it may refer to the ability of texts to be transferred from one object to the next without a loss of information. Unlike the corpse, which remains irreplaceable, the *corpus* that an individual leaves behind does not depend on the duration of a *particular* material manifestation. This is one of the keys to the longevity of texts. Despite the thousands of copies of the Bible that stand between us, the Bible that I read today consists of the same narrative that was written down by the authors of the Gospels centuries ago, which is (supposedly) an extension of the very actions and words of Christ himself. The *Epic of Gilgamesh* in your bookshelf (provided you own a copy of the old Sumerian version) contains the same story it did thousands of years ago. What has changed is the form, the physical manifestation of the story, not the content. When information is portable, the surface on which it is inscribed becomes replaceable, although, as we shall see throughout this book, it is not insignificant.

On the other hand, portability may refer to the fact that the written word can transport memories across space like no other technology before it. Before writing, any information stored outside of the human brain was as good as immobile, meaning that memories and ancestral identity remained spatially confined. If your ancestors are represented by houses, statues, or large erected stones, you do not just move them around without further ado. There are exceptions, to be sure, like the relocation of Stonehenge. In Neolithic Britain, stone was deeply associated with the ancestors. (In fact, it was strictly reserved for the dwellings of the dead. The living had to make do with perishable materials like wood). The Stonehenge rocks are hence thought to have symbolized the ancestral community or even to have been considered to *be* the ancestors. The bluestones that make up the monument's outer circle, each approximately 2–3 meters tall, were moved some 200 kilometers from Preseli Hills in Wales to the Salisbury Plain in England; this massive effort should be interpreted as nothing short of a transportation of ancestral authority, an attempt to preserve the migrants' relationship to their past so as to keep intact the union between the living and the dead (and, by implication, uniting the living as a group of common origin).[21] Stonehenge may be ever so impressive, yet most people, I believe, would prefer to simply bring their ancestors along in the form of inscriptions on tablets, or, indeed, *paper*, rather than human-sized rocks.

The memory of the dead only travels as far and as fast as

the material on which it is inscribed or projected. Writing on clay tablets, therefore, afforded a huge push toward disseminating legacies across vast spatial distances. To connect with ritual forms of remembering, as explained by German Egyptologist Jan Assman, "you have to go to an image, a monument, a sacred place in order to reconnect with its meaning." To connect with the meaning of written cultural texts, on the other hand, "you simply have to read them."[22] When the worship of a founder-ancestor is fixed in writing, it is no longer confined to groups of people who consider themselves kin but can be spread across geographical boundaries. The global dissemination of world religions like Islam and Christianity are a testament to this. The only reason a Christian from modern-day Sri Lanka can feel kinship with one from, say, fifteenth-century Norway, despite neither probably ever having visited Judea or even set foot on the same soil as each other, is because they have both read (or listened) to the words of the same long-dead founder. Such a community across space and time is unimaginable without the scriptures, the prosthetic voices, that define them. The written word, thus, *liberated* the dead from their corporeal fixation in time and space. Instead of merely existing as immobile bodies of (rotting) flesh, a *corpse*, the dead were granted a new mobile body—a *corpus* inscribed into tablets of clay or scrolls of papyrus.

Writing is not the only technology to separate the dead person from their corporeal presence. It merely exemplifies a quality that can generally be found in any form of information technology. Consider photography as a more recent example. In his classic essay *Camera Lucida*, Roland Barthes calls the invention of photography a "cunning dissociation of consciousness from identity."[23] In the photograph, says

Barthes, the identity of a person is dislocated from the space where the conscious mind resides (the biological body); it assumes an existence independent of the flesh. The photograph separates *being as a person* from *being as a conscious agent*. This is why photography is so intimately connected to death. The individuals in the old photographs that Barthes studies are present in an absurd way; looking at the photos, he sees people who have their whole lives ahead of them, and yet those people are probably dead *already*. The individuals featured in the photographs are real and present in that they are extensions of actual persons. Yet they are not alive. They are dead, both in the biological sense (they cannot possibly be alive by the time their images reach Barthes) and also in the sense that photography inevitably portrays objects as stale and inanimate by freezing them in the moment. This gap between the real and the living, as Barthes has it, is why the essence, the *eidos*, of photography is death.

As with writing—or perhaps with all new information technologies?—photography is empirically connected to the dead. Immediately upon Louis Daguerre's presentation of the first so-called daguerreotypes (what we today refer to as photographs), corpses became some of the most popular motifs.[24] Families throughout the Western world, especially in the Anglophone parts, would typically bring the corpse of a deceased family member (particularly children) to a photographer to have a portrait of the corpse taken before it started to decompose. The corpse would often be portrayed as sleeping but would sometimes be posed as if alive. Although portraits of actual corpses were soon surpassed in popularity by living motifs, photography remained an important mediator of the dead. Prior to the photographic revolution, for spatially distant people to possess a representation of your face, even before it went into the ground, would have been an expensive endeavor requiring a painter or a sculptor. As a considerably cheaper alternative, photography thus democratized access to a posthumous presence. In fact, only decades after its invention, photos of deceased family members became a standard part of interiors among middle-class families in the US and parts of Europe, which, according to historian Elizabeth Hallam and sociologist Jenny Hockey, turned the domestic environment into "a site of materialized memory . . . conducive to personal reflection and remembering."[25] Not unlike the skulls kept in Natufian houses, or the *imago* mask of Ancient Rome, photographs once again adorned the walls of the house with the faces of the dead.

Another notable mediator of the dead is the telegraph. As vividly described by cultural historian Jeffery Sconce, this invention sparked an entire movement, Spiritualism, around the idea that electronic communications could somehow reach the afterlife world and bring back all kinds of messages from the dead. Samuel Morse, the inventor of the telegraph, was allegedly a particularly frequent interlocutor after his death, as reported by many of Spiritualism's practitioners. It is easy to ridicule such beliefs today, but the fact is that many of the most prominent scientists of the nineteenth century were firm believers in the possibility of communicating with the dead through electronic media. In a way, it all made sense. As Sconce explains:[26]

> The Spiritualists' initial conceptualization of "celestial telegraphy" was not so much a misapplication of technological discourse as a logical elaboration of the technology's already "supernatural" characteristics. Talking with the dead through raps and knocks, after all, was only slightly more miraculous

> than talking with the living yet absent through dots and dashes; both involved subjects reconstituted through technology as an entity at once interstitial and uncanny.

In other words, the telegraph, and later also other technologies like wireless radio and TV, *decoupled* personal presence from the confines of the body, allowing for a disembodied communication that could transcend both time and space. And insofar as the presence of the body becomes redundant for communication, its demise (i.e., death) ceases to matter—the immortal mind/soul can live on in the ether and the ether can be accessed by electronic communications. Or at least so reasoned the Spiritualists.

The lesson here is that all information technologies decouple the dead from their biological confines. It is their very nature. Whether in the form of houses, letters, or photographs, technology provides us with prosthetic bodies, voices, and faces. And these new bodies, if rightly built, survive the flesh and can travel great distances in time and space. Yet, despite these liberating qualities, they are, nevertheless, *containers*. Whether in a grave, book, record, or photo album, the dead are always *in* something, an enclosed space framed off from the outside world.[27] Books and photo albums have covers not only to protect them from damage but to mark the line where the past ends and the present begins. Herein lies the irony of portability: the very thing that enables the liberation of the dead from their physical remains is also what enables the separation between the living and the dead in society. When the dead reside right under your feet, they will remain there, whether you like it or not. But as the actual corpse is replaced by a corpus inscribed on paper, it can always be placed *elsewhere*. Technology, that is, separates the deceased person from their biological body and thereby also facilitates a separation of the dead from the spaces occupied by the living. It leaves it to the living to decide where to place a deceased person's information. Stone tablets and books helped Gilgamesh survive for thousands of years, but they are also strikingly simple to stuff away in a dusty library, far from the world of the living. Let me elaborate.

The Port from Which We Depart

On May 1, 1873, the Italian anatomist Lodovico Brunetti presented a new machine to the world. He called it "Crémation des Cadavres." It was an outrageous, even sacrilegious machine, whose simple yet awe-inspiring purpose was to transform the cadaver of a fully grown human into nothing more than a cup of ash. It fulfilled its promise with stunning speed. In a matter of a few hours, 45 kilos of human flesh and bones were reduced to merely 1.77 kilos of pure cinder. Though this accomplishment may not seem especially impressive—after all, funeral pyres had existed in various European and Asian cultures for millennia—this first specimen of the modern cremation furnace was the herald of an entirely new thanatological regime. It was the harbinger of annihilation.

The 1873 prototype was not Brunetti's first attempt. On the contrary, it was the product of years of trial and error. His first, built in 1869, had an open brick furnace fueled by walnut wood. Though it managed to transform a 55-kilogram woman into 2.5 kilos of calcined bones in a matter of only four hours, its results were ultimately unsatisfactory. The incineration was not complete but had left small pieces of bone in the ashes. In January of 1870, Brunetti made a second experiment, involving a rack of perforated iron on which he had placed pieces of a chopped-up body, but this too failed to live up to his expectations. And so did attempts three and four. It was not until he implemented sophisticated technology from the steel industry, where heat is generated through reverberation of gases, that he ultimately succeeded. The final cremation furnace, the one presented in Vienna in 1873, could generate temperatures of up to 1100°C, enough to transform even the smallest pieces of bone into dust and gas. And so Brunetti's mission was complete: his Crémation des Cadavres transformed dead people into virtually nothing.

Brunetti's manic determination to enable a complete incineration of the dead illustrates the contrast between the modern cremation movement and its historical precedents. People have been burning their departed kin for millennia. The ancient Greeks did it (for the most part). So did the Romans in the Late Republic. Some of the Vikings were cremated, too. It was not totally uncommon among Neolithic cultures. Buddhists and Hindus have practiced cremation for millennia without interruption. But in each of these cases, burning the dead represents a means to bring them honor. It was because the dead were cared for that they were burned. The modern cremation movement, on the other hand, was not driven by courtesy or tradition but ultimately represented a progression of reason and science. As put by Laqueur, cremation "represented the maximum modernist programme of nineteenth-century science in the face of death, indeed in the face of all humanity." It was hailed by its advocates as a "final triumph of reason and common sense"—the ultimate manifestation of enlightenment.[28]

What made cremation so "rational?" Sir Henry Thompson, a bit of a nineteenth-century science rock star who had been much impressed with Brunetti's invention, had many answers to that question. Only months after he had first seen the demonstration in Vienna, he founded the British Cremation Society, which would play a crucial role in advocating the modern way of dealing with the dead. Among the many alleged benefits of cremation was hygiene. Thompson saw leaving the dead to decompose in the ground, as was the tradition in Christian Europe, as a cause of all kinds of diseases. To avoid these, he advised the living to get rid of the dead altogether. Another benefit was space efficiency. An urn of ash is considerably smaller than a human-sized coffin and thus does not demand as much cemetery space. The extra space could be used for the rapid expansion of cities. Traditional burial also represented a terrible economic waste. In the 1870s, an average of 80,430 people died in Greater London each year, and almost all of them were buried. Combined, their bodies represented 206,282 pounds of ash, which is an excellent fertilizer with a considerable market value. On this basis, Thompson argued that Britain hoarded hundreds of thousands of British pounds underground (hundreds of millions in today's terms), where it was not put to any economic use. "Capital is intended to bear good interest," he said, suggesting that, since it certainly did not do the dead any good anymore, the biological capital of their bodies ought to serve the living instead. The goal of the cremation movement was, in other words, not merely to annihilate the dead but to make them work for the living, to recruit them in what Laqueur calls "a regime of life."[29]

A similar tendency can also be observed in the development of other death-related technologies that emerged during the latter half of the nineteenth century. Even crafts like photography and medical embalming, which are intuitively means to *preserve* the dead among the living, became part of a larger mission to suspend death from the human body and to succumb the dead into the circulation of capital, to paraphrase John Troyer, director of the Centre for Death and Society at the University of Bath. In his book *Technologies of the Human Corpse*, Troyer describes how the technological leap of the nineteenth century allowed an entire new industry to emerge around the dead, turning the human cadaver into an "unfettered source of capital."[30] The dead, argues Troyer, were no longer merely dead but reinvented and manufactured as a consumer product. Indeed, in modernity, the dead are above all subject to the regime of life.

It is striking how well the death-related technologies of the nineteenth century in general, and the cremation movement in particular, resonate with the larger ideals of modernity. For what is modernity if not an attempt to rid society of its dependence on the past, to liberate it from the traditions and irrational habits of the old and replace them with the rational and new? And what can be a better personification of the past than its inhabitants—the dead? As phrased by the French historian Philippe Ariès in his pioneering *Western Attitudes toward Death*, the modern age is above all an era of "forbidden death," an excommunication of the dead from the public sphere.[31] Indeed, even the very word *modern* comes from the Latin *modo*, meaning "right now" or "the present." Death in modernity must be hidden and avoided, argues Ariès, no longer for the sake of the dying person but primarily "for the sake of society." He continues, "It is above all essential that society—the neighbours, friends, colleagues and children—notice to the least possible degree that death has occurred."[32] Modern cultures do not all cremate their dead in a literal sense; in the United States, for example, only about 50 percent of dead bodies are cremated. But although not every body may be physically incinerated, they are all nevertheless figuratively erased in the sense that their presence in public affairs loses its validity. The dead must be gone. Modernity is, in other words, the ultimate manifestation of the aforementioned separation between the living and the dead afforded by increasing portability of the latter. The written word made it possible to stuff the dead away in archives and bookshelves. The cremation furnace completed the process by removing them completely from the face of the earth. As the sociologist Zygmunt Bauman summarizes it, modernity "killed death."[33] At least it tried to.

The modern assault on the dead is also a political project. It plays a key role, implicitly and explicitly, in each of the major ideologies of modern politics. Consider liberalism. It is not by coincidence that in the American Declaration of Independence—a document with unparalleled significance, not only to liberalism but to the entire modern political order—Thomas Jefferson chooses *life*, *liberty* and the *pursuit of happiness* as the cardinal virtues of the state, instead of, say, dignity, honor, and tradition. Notably, both liberty and happiness, and obviously also *life*, are goods that exclusively befall living individuals, in contrast to alternative political subjects. Years later, Jefferson would even explicate this stance in a letter in which he states that "the earth belongs in usufruct to the living" while the dead "have neither powers nor rights over it."[34] Liberalism, and its interpretation of the role of the state in society, is, in other words, exclusively a project for the living, the rightful proprietors of the earth. By contrast to the religious, aristocratic, and feudal political systems that preceded it, liberal society is through and through a "regime of life."[35]

In contemporary Western societies, this liberal regime has

primarily manifested in two fundamental social institutions: liberal democracy and the free market. Both are systems explicitly in service of the present population. In democratic states, only the living can vote. Hence, the living are the only ones worth convincing, the only ones whose interests are worth consideration—at the expense of both past and future generations, whose membership in the *demos* is either yet to be or no longer. There is a counterpoint to be made in that democracy, at least in its liberal Western interpretation, is, on the contrary, the dominance of *past* generations over the present. We abide, after all, by laws that were sometimes made long before our lifetimes. The United States, for instance, is still tightly bound by a constitution whose authors have been dead for centuries. Yet the fact that this is generally regarded as a flaw, rather than a feature, of democracy is telling for how we moderns conceive of it. The argument is that in abiding by laws made by the dead, democracy fails to live up to its promise, which implicitly means that this promise is a promise of complete dominance of the present.

The market, similarly, gives power only to present consumers. Unless you have capital to spend, you are nothing. The worth of your interests can be measured in dollars and cents, and since neither future nor past generations are considered natural persons, they have no such resources at hand. Here, one could make the case that the (capitalist) market is a dominance of the future rather than the present. The reason that we collectively work many more hours than is needed to sustain ourselves is because of the fear of *tomorrow*. In capitalism, those who do not invest for tomorrow will soon be out of the game. And so, whatever is consumed today is a lost investment for tomorrow. Hence, we are all, workers and capitalists alike, slaves of the future. There is certainly some truth to this, and I shall return to the mechanisms of capitalism in more detail in both chapters 3 and 4. Yet, ultimately, this so-called dominance of the future does no good for its actual inhabitants. Indeed, this requirement to constantly invest and make the economy grow ultimately results in a consumption of natural resources at the expense of future generations. The market may be investing for the future, but it is surely not shaping a society for future well-being. At best, it is shaping society according to the will of instant consumers.

Socialism bears the same stamp of disdain for the past. For Karl Marx, whose influence on socialist thought cannot be matched by any other thinker, the influence of past generations on contemporary society was at best a superstition and at worst an obstacle to true emancipation. "The tradition of all dead generations," he complains in *The Eighteenth Brumaire of Louis Bonaparte*, "weighs like a nightmare on the brains of the living."[36] To realize the revolution, this yoke of the dead must be shaken off. Though we should not blame Marx, or even socialism, for the confused interpretations that emerged in the Soviet Union and China during the twentieth century, this hostility toward the dead remains clearly visible in their rhetoric and politics. Consider the revolutionary poetry of Russian futurist Vladimir Mayakovsky, a key voice during the formative years of the Bolshevik party. In 1917, Mayakovsky, together with fellow poets and artists David Burliuk, Aleksei Kruchenykh, and Viktor Khlebnikov, published one of his most explicitly political poems, entitled "A Slap in the Face of Good Taste."[37] Already in its opening lines, the authors make clear that modernity has no place for the dead:

> *We* alone was the *face* of *our* Time. Through us the horn of time blows in the art of the world.

> The past is too tight. The Academy and Pushkin are less intelligible than hieroglyphics.
>
> Throw Pushkin, Dostoevsky, Tolstoy, etc., etc. overboard from the Ship of Modernity.
>
> He who does not forget his *first* love will not recognize his last.
>
> All those Maxim Gorkys, Krupins, Bloks, Sologubs, Remizovs, Averchenkos, Chornys, Kuzmins, Bunins, etc. need only a dacha on the river. Such is the reward fate gives tailors.
>
> From the heights of skyscrapers we gaze at their insignificance! . . .

There is an irony in that in order to throw Pushkin, Dostoevsky, and Tolstoy "off the ship of modernity," the futurist poets needed to bring them along in the first place. In fact, these young men were almost obsessed with the giants of the golden age of Russian literature that preceded them. (Allegedly, the first thing Mayakovsky did upon his release from prison in 1910 was to resume reading Tolstoy's *Anna Karenina*). In any case, the futurist poets' explicit denouncing of the (dead) masters of old is indicative not only of the literary project of the radical circles around Mayakovsky but of the general mission of socialism. The most extreme manifestation of this mission is the brutality of the Cultural Revolution in China, commencing in 1966, in which virtually any artifact inhabited by the memory of the dead was destroyed in a war against the "four old"—old customs, culture, habits, and ideas. One may counter that both the Soviet Union and communist China, and even more so pseudo-socialist states like North Korea, are in fact obsessed with the dead. Afterall, the embalmed corpse of Vladimir Lenin had (and has) an almost sacred status, and the worship of departed leaders like Mao Zedong and Kim Il-sung (who remains the "eternal President of the Republic") has an almost necrocratic undertone. Yet, insofar as so-called socialist countries worship the dead, their doing so should be understood as a *failure* to realize their socialist ideals. Without some serious intellectual acrobatics, it cannot be justified within the paradigm of socialist thought.

The point here is that, whether liberal or socialist, the modern political order is essentially a form of conceptual cremation in a furnace of ideas rather than flesh. It is a forever moving steamboat for which the dead are only granted a ticket in order to be thrown off.

Critics of modernity, especially those who fall within the conservative camp, have criticized its hostility toward the nonliving for centuries. The earliest and fiercest among these is Edmund Burke, commonly hailed as the father of conservative thought.[38] In contrast to other thinkers of his time, such as Jefferson—who, as we saw, disregards any influence of the dead on society—Burke sees the dead as a fundamental part of the social contract, as natural, even necessary members of society. To Burke, what binds social groups together over time is not merely a contract between the individual and the collective (as for Hobbes) but a contract spanning across generations, or, as he puts it, "a partnership not only between those who are living, but between those who are living, those who are dead, and those who are to be born."[39] To be a conservative, in the Burkean sense, is thus to facilitate and maintain balance within the partnership by preserving the virtues and resources of the past generation for the benefit of future ones. Several contemporary thinkers have developed Burke's notion of the social contract further. Harvard historian Niall Ferguson, for instance, has argued that the current economic regime is stealing from future generations in order to give to the present.[40] The English conservative philosopher Roger Scruton similarly argues that the liberal paradigm privileges the living members of society at the expense of the nonliving members of the "partnership."[41] Yet, Burke's notion of the social contract does not require an endorsement of conservatism as a political project (especially not as it is enacted today, which is arguably the opposite of the ideas accounted for above). In the context of this book, the notion of a "tyranny of the present" merely suggests that modernity is far from morally neutral when it comes to nonliving generations. Toward the final chapter, I shall return to this notion to discuss how it may help us formulate a response to the ethical challenges of living in the post-mortal condition.

Modernity as a project is intrinsically hostile to the dead. None of this, however, is to say that people who live in modern societies do not care for their departed kin. Of course they do. Anyone who has ever lost a loved one knows that the ties that connect us with one another are not broken even by death. We continue to *care* for the dead. We fulfill their wishes, take care of their bodies, respect their wills, even if we know well that there would be no repercussions from their side If we did not. Funeral homes have been more prosperous than ever during the twentieth century, finding increasingly novel ways of selling their products—new and ever more expensive coffins, floral ornaments, paperwork management, and so on. Personal genealogy research prospers, as more and more people seek to find out about their families' pasts. Indeed, the dead do remain within the emotional life of the bereaved. Yet, in modernity, these dealings with the dead are viewed as an exclusively *private* matter. To the modern individual, grief is a process that consists of stages, where the final destination is to find "closure," to return to a normalcy where the absurdity of death cannot reach us.[42] It is in this context that a technology like the cremation furnace must be understood. Its goal is not merely to annihilate the corpse, but to restore order, and to recruit the dead to the only regime that can possibly matter: the regime of life to which the earth, and everything on it, belongs.

This regime is the backdrop against which we should interpret the digital disruption of our way of being with the dead. It is from this port that we depart.

Where Are We Now?

It is hard to pin down an exact position, let alone a direction of travel, in times of rapid change. Indeed, describing how our relationship to the dead is changing, and how we can become active agents in this process, will require the remainder of this book. But placing it in the historical context of previous technological disruptions makes things a little clearer. It allows us to set some basic frames to the narrative of where we are and where we are going in terms of our relationship to the dead.

On some level, the narrative is fairly self-explanatory given the basic facts. More than 2.2 billion people are expected to pass away within the next three decades alone.[43] And if internet penetration rates keep rising at their current rate, most of these will leave some kind of online presence behind. As I discuss in more detail in the following chapter, there is even a realistic chance that the dead will outnumber the living on

Facebook within only four decades, meaning that our daily venues for communication are increasingly shared with the dead. Meanwhile, the kind of media that the dead leave behind are able to preserve ever larger amounts of information, so that the line separating their world from ours becomes increasingly vague. In short, in the information society, the dead are everywhere. So far so good, but placing these numbers in a historical context helps us see further. First and foremost, we see that the emergence of the dead online is more than a mere matter for the bereaved or a headache for online platforms. The first houses were once dwellings for both the living and the dead, symbols of what it means to live in human civilization. Today, the internet is becoming the house in which society takes place. Placed in this context, the online presence of the dead emerges as a harbinger of civilizational disruption.[44] What is at stake is our very relationship to our collective past and its inhabitants and, ultimately, to ourselves as a species. We also see that digital technologies are not unique in their ability to preserve the dead among us. On the contrary, they are a continuation of techno-cultural practices as old as the *Epic of Gilgamesh*, the most recent chapter in the project of decoupling the dead person from their biological confines. Digital media is, like all information technologies before it, part of a construction of a *portable* prosthetic body. What was once a corpus of letters is inscribed as ones and zeroes.[45] Finally, we see the techno-cultural backdrop against which the current development is taking place: the hidden death of modernity.[46] Everything I describe in this book will be in contrast to it. For this reason, I shall refer to our new (or not so new?) mode of being with the dead as a *post-mortal condition*, as an homage to Jean-François Lyotard's notion of the post*modern* condition.[47] Post-mortal, however, does not mean that the digital is somehow immortal (in fact, it is exceptionally fragile) but that society now takes place in a domain that, under modernity, has been reserved for the dead: the archives. In the digital age, where recording has become the default and the past is perfectly portable, we live in and through an almost perfect record of the past. Even our smallest actions leave some trace behind, and those traces now constitute our social environment just as much as the physical houses and cities where we reside.[48] Once again, we are beginning to live with the dead *around* us.

So, this is the story of where we are and how we got here. But none of this *determines* how we choose to live with the dead. Cultures always find their own ways to deal with their pasts, and so our options at the cusp of the digital age remain as open as they ever were. The question is where we *choose* to go from here—what do we do with the dead now that they emerge among us, and how do we make this *our* choice?

2 * How to Think about Digital Remains

> If I am, then death is not. If death is, then I am not. Why should I fear that which can only exist when I do not?
>
> **Epicurus**

> I would as willingly see Brutus in Plutarch, as in a book of his own. I would rather choose to be certainly informed of the conference he had in his tent with some particular friends of his the night before a battle, than of the harangue he made the next day to his army; and of what he did in his closet and his chamber, than what he did in the public square and in the senate.
>
> **Michel de Montaigne**

What Are Digital Remains?

On July 12, 2018, the Federal Court of Justice in Karlsruhe, Germany's highest court for civil and criminal law, made a landmark decision. The case concerned the tragic story of a fifteen-year-old girl who had been killed by a train at a Berlin train station six years earlier. With the police unable to determine whether the incident had been an accident or a suicide, the bereaved parents had turned to the girl's Facebook account for clarity. Was there perhaps something in their daughter's correspondences that would give them some clues? To their great dismay, someone had already reported the girl dead and "memorialized" her profile, a feature implemented by Facebook as an option for profiles of deceased users (I will talk about it at length in chapter 3). This meant that the original information in the profile could not be accessed, even with the account password. Facebook refused to open the profile again, partly citing the privacy of those with whom the girl had communicated. An initial ruling gave the parents the right to go forth with their request, but in 2017, this ruling was reversed by a Berlin state court that sided with Facebook. The final 2018 ruling, however, reversed it again and sided with the parents. Part of the reason given was that while the European Union's General Data Protection Regulation (GDPR) is one of the world's strongest protections of individual users' privacy, all such rights cease at the moment of death. Dead people have no right to privacy. In its final statement, the court thus declared that it regarded digital communications as no different from physical objects like letters or diaries, and that the parents were consequently entitled to *inherit* their daughter's digital remains, including the messages sent to her by other Facebook users.

This tragic episode illustrates the complexities of managing privacy law in the face of death. But it also sheds light on a more fundamental question, namely: What exactly are "digital remains?"

In a concrete sense, the answer is rather obvious—digital remains are whatever data we leave behind: Facebook profiles, Spotify playlists and preferences, Google search histories, Zoom logs, emails, video game avatars, chat logs, photo libraries, and so on. Fair enough, but as soon as we introduce any sort of common name to refer to these various forms of data, we need to step into the realm of the metaphoric. For whenever we talk about the intangible things that appear on our screens, we do so with reference to the tangible world we know from tactile experience. On the "web," we go to different "sites" where we may download "files" that we put in "folders" on our "desktops." There is no such thing as a physical file inside your computer, and your desktop does not correspond to any location inside it. Yet "file" and "desktop" remain useful heuristics for thinking about and structuring the information you receive from the device.

The reason we need to connect the intangible world with tangible precedents is that the latter already have a catalog of social and cultural protocols around them that serve as instructions for how to behave around and interact with them. I know that when I am invited to someone's room or house, courtesy requires that I follow *their* rules. So, when I am invited to a Zoom "room," I already have some preconception of how to behave when I am "in there." Unlike in a phone call, I am a "guest" and someone else will be "host," and while these titles may seem arbitrary, they do an important job in providing certain expectations and (moral) responsibilities—a protocol for how to behave and act.

The same is true for the data we leave behind after we die. To even begin discussing our responsibilities—what we ought to do with them—we must connect them to some concrete *thing* in the tangible world. Only then can we begin making sense of our situation. There is reason to choose our metaphors carefully. Just as labels like "host" and "guest" come with certain expectations and responsibilities, so does the label we choose for dead people's data structure our ethical responsibilities toward those people. For instance, when the German court sided with the parents in the above case, they did so explicitly by reference to how we deal with tangible objects like diaries and letters. In addition, the academic literature has produced wide-ranging vocabulary for talking about dead peoples' data, including "digital ghosts," "digital estates," "digital human remains," "online angels," and "digital zombies," to name a few.[1] It is not my intention to promote any of these as better or worse than another (not even the court's comparison to "diaries"). As a matter of fact, I happen to believe that complex phenomena like the disruption of the bedrock of civilization (i.e., our relationship to the dead) require more conceptual tools, not fewer. Yet, two metaphors are key to the larger argument posed in this book: the *body* and the *encyclopedia*. The former because it offers a bridge to existing debates on posthumous harm; the latter because it illustrates the inevitably *collective* nature of digital remains. Let us look closer at each.

Ghost Cars and Prayer Bots

There is a YouTube clip uploaded by PBS Game/Show entitled "Can Video Games Be a Spiritual Experience?" The content of the video itself is insignificant, at least for the purpose of this book. But in one of the 2385 comments posted to the video, user 00WARTHERAPY00 shares an episode from his life that highlights a central aspect of how digital technology shapes our relationship to the dead. I quote it verbatim below:

> Well, when i was 4, my dad bought a trusty xBox. you know, the first, ruggedy, blocky one from 2001. we had tons and tons and tons of fun playing all kinds of games together—until he died, when i was just 6.
>
> i couldnt touch that console for 10 years.
>
> but once i did, i noticed something.
>
> we used to play a racing game, Rally Sports Challenge. actually pretty awesome for the time it came.
>
> and once i started meddling around . . . i found a GHOST.
>
> literaly.

> you know, when a time race happens, that the fastest lap so far gets recorded as a ghost driver? yep, you guessed it—his ghost still rolls around the track today.
>
> and so i played and played, and played, untill i was almost able to beat the ghost. until one day i got ahead of it, i surpassed it, and . . . ~
>
> i stopped right in front of the finish line, just to ensure i wouldnt delete it.
>
> Bliss.

This simple yet heartwarming story struck a chord. At the time of this writing, the comment has well over twenty-six thousand likes and almost five hundred subcomments celebrating it. It even became the basis for a short film by American filmmaker John Wikstrom.[2]

Part of what makes the episode so intriguing is that 00WARTHERAPY00's story is more than a comment about the spiritual element of video games. It also illustrates the interactive nature of our digital footprints. Ten years after the father's death, a shard of his agency still remains present, frozen like crystal within the console. Though he has assumed the shape of a computer game avatar, it is still possible to compete with *him*, as if he had just passed over the controller a second ago. Put the metaphysical aspects aside for a second—the father is still *there*, insofar as the son is concerned.

The ghost car in Rally Sports Challenge contains only *one* crystalized trace of the individual who was once 00WARTHERAPY00's father, and a rather simplistic one at that. It tells us hardly anything about who he was, except perhaps as a video game rally driver. By contrast, the traces left behind even by the most modest internet user contain a flood of information, possibly including materials the user was completely unaware of (like cookies and geodata), and probably some things they would not want anyone else to ever lay their eyes on (most people, I reckon, would probably not want their children to inherit their search data). But just as the ghost car of Rally Sports Challenge carries a shard of the departed father's play, so do your data effectively become an imprint of *you*. Your social media profile embodies your way of socializing: your way with words; how often you reach out to people, and to whom; how fast you respond to messages, and whether you tend to ignore them for a while; what kind of items you tend to click on, and what you scroll past; and so on. Your playlists reveal what kind of music you listen to, and when. Your credit card data says a lot about what makes you pick up your wallet. What you watch on YouTube gives a pretty accurate picture of what grabs your attention. And there are a lot of these data. In 2020, the global data production per capita was 1.7 MB per second.[3] Not all of those data are personal, of course, and most of them are deleted almost immediately upon generation. But the number gives some indication, if ever so vague, of just how much information we leave behind.

There is, however, a nontrivial difference between the video game race and the "raw" data people leave behind on the web. The former is an interactive software that "animates" the actions of the dead; the latter remains frozen just the way it was left. Yet the distinction is increasingly blurred. In 2016, Russian AI programmer Eugenia Kuyda announced the launch of a new app she had been working on, called Roman Mazurenko: A Digital Avatar. Mazurenko was a close friend to Eugenia who had passed away in a tragic car accident a year earlier, leaving behind some 8000 lines of text messages with Eugenia alone. Eugenia decided that the best way to honor her late friend was to preserve him in the form of an interactive bot. Drawing upon her AI project Luka, she used her correspondence with Roman as input to train an interactive entity that would behave, if not exactly like Roman, at least as a version of him—a shard of his personality. It is still available on App Store today. And like the ghost car preserved OOWARTHERAPYOO's father as a rally driver, it still holds a shard of Roman Mazurenko, at least as a text-message conversation partner. As our digital footprints grow ever larger, and as the technological means become increasingly accessible—the machine learning system that helped replicate Roman, TensorFlow, has been made available open-source by Google—plenty of similar examples have emerged, from virtual-reality encounters with deceased children to social networks for the dead. I shall write about these at length in the next chapter, but for now, let us just note that digital remains are becoming increasingly animated.

Not all automation of a person's posthumous presence needs to be that high-tech, though. For illustration, let me elaborate for a moment on the case of the increasingly popular Islamic prayer apps. The business plan of Islamic prayer apps is as simple as it is innovative. Muslims commonly engage in religious supplication (دُعاء, *du'a*), a humble request for an event to occur or a wish to be fulfilled. Believers may phrase their own personal supplications, but there is also an array of examples in the Quran to choose from. Unlike the mandatory five-times-a-day prayer that is normally associated with Islam, supplications can be automated—at least according to apps. The site Du3a.org, on which I led a study in 2018, is a typical example: The site's landing page features some Quranic quotes and popular prayers, and a sidebar encourages visitors to share the site on different social networks like Facebook and Pinterest, claiming that twenty-six million visitors have done so already. But the most salient feature is perhaps the button prompting visitors to subscribe to the service. Upon doing so, visitors are redirected to X (formerly Twitter), where they are asked to authorize Du3a.org to use their account and post on their behalf. If a visitor accepts, Du3a.org begins to automatically post a <140-character supplication from their account every second hour, alongside a site URL (and until recently, a "recycling" emoji). According to our study, there are at least ten sites with business models similar to that of Du3a.org, though some of the competitors offer more advanced options. Athantweets.com, for instance, offers a premium version that, for 100 Saudi riyals (roughly $27) a year, enables users to choose specific (as opposed to randomly generated) supplications, and to synchronize the tweets to their local prayer times. Tweets sent via this premium package also hide the Athantweets URL, making them virtually indistinguishable from any other tweets with Islamic content, and unidentifiable by bot-detection software. During the same day, a single user might post one tweet about politics, a second one containing a supplication, and a third one complaining about the long lines in airport security. For an unfamiliar audience, there would be no chance of telling that only the first and the last were literally posted by the user themselves, while the middle one was sent by a script.

All this may seem rather baffling to secular readers, but what exactly does it have to do with the dead? The answer lies in the eschatology of Islam. Unlike many other religions, Islam holds that in the time between a person's death and the final judgment day, there are a number of factors that can increase that person's standing in the eyes of God. According to one of the seminal Islamic hadiths (a form of canonical religious witness statement about what Muhammed said and did that is not part of the Quran), the Prophet Muhammed specifically mentioned three such things: the continuous effects of charity, the provision of knowledge to be used by future generations, and having virtuous descendants who pray for you.[4] Because contributing to the dissemination of Islam online is considered an inherent good, it is less important whether this activity is performed by someone personally or through knowledge that one helps disseminate. So, setting up an app to post supplications on one's behalf after death could help increase one's chances of a good afterlife. It is not unlike an Islamic version of Catholic indulgences, only the prayers are sent out from social media bots rather than clergy. To our surprise, we found that nearly all Islamic prayer apps stress this angle explicitly by marketing their product with references to the afterlife. The slogan of Zad-Muslim.com, for instance, reads "Register now so your account will tweet now and after you die," and Du3a.org promises that "your account will tweet in your life and in your death," to name but two examples. During our aforementioned study, we even discovered accounts dedicated solely to reenforcing the posthumous piety of deceased family members.

Our biggest surprise, however, was not the frequency of references to the afterlife but the spread of the phenomenon. Du3a.org is presumably one of the largest Islamic prayer apps, and it is also one of the easiest to study, since it includes the same URL in every tweet it posts from users' profiles. Using Twitter's "firehose," a function which then gave access to everything posted on Twitter (under certain criteria) during a given time frame, my co-authors and I downloaded every tweet containing the Du3a.org URL during a forty-eight-hour period. Over these two days, the script collected no less than 3.8 million tweets—1.9 million per day (!). Let me put that in context. Four years prior to our collection of the Du3a.org data, a report estimated that the entire Arabic-speaking Twitter encompassed approximately 17.2 million tweets per day, meaning that Du3a.org alone would account for roughly one in every ten tweets posted in Arabic (provided this estimate was still relevant).[5] During the Arab Spring, on the day when Egyptian President Hosni Mubarak resigned, the hashtag #egypt got around 205,000 tweets. And that was on its busiest day. One may also compare the popularity of Du3a.org to other forms of automated content. For example, in the 2016 US election, when significant popular attention focused on the role of automated accounts, a study by data scientists Alessandro Bessi and Emilio Ferrara estimated that a maximum of 3.8 million tweets on political topics had come from automated accounts in the week leading up to Election Day (an average of about 540,000 tweets per day).[6] In other words, according to our analysis, a single automated prayer app generated as many tweets in two days as automated accounts generated about the 2016 US presidential election in the whole week leading up to Election Day.[7] Yet, Du3a.org keeps on posting every day of the year, and it is but one among many similar apps. No one knows the total count of tweets such apps generate, especially since some of them leave no trace of automation. But even the traffic from Du3a.org alone is big enough to shift metrics of the entire platform, and slowly but surely, this traffic is being posted by accounts that belong to deceased users. In a couple of decades, the dead may be responsible for one of the biggest social phenomena on X (Twitter), at least in terms of sheer number of posts.

The Islamic prayer apps display how an automated digital afterlife presence does not necessarily have to be very high-tech. Aspects of one's social or religious presence can be automated with relatively simple means yet grant (at least the promise of) an eternal presence. They also show that we may answer PBS Game/Show's question in the affirmative—video games, and more importantly social media, *can* be a spiritual experience. For the users of Islamic prayer apps, it evidently is. The digital afterlife phenomenon, then, is not limited to a few tech-savvy enthusiasts in Silicon Valley. It is a spiritual low-tech phenomenon around the world. Also, like the Xbox ghost car, Islamic prayer apps illustrate that informational remains are not merely stale matter but continue to act in the social worlds of our descendants. But how we should think about these agencies? What *are* they? And what will they become as our technologies, and the data they collect, grow ever more sophisticated and comprehensive? These are big questions, rooted in our very understanding of the nature of data. They need answers before we go about examining the ethical and political implications.

The Informational Corpse

According to some people, it is simple: automation technology is the first step toward digital immortality. The AI that drives it is not merely metaphorical, it is the seed to a full replication of the human brain. Soon, our personal data records will be so comprehensive, and our AI so sophisticated, that the demise of one's biological body will be a mere detail.

People who hold this view typically refer to themselves as "transhumanists."[8] Transhumanism is, in the words of its most prominent advocator, philosopher Nick Bostrom, a loosely defined movement that "promotes an interdisciplinary approach to understanding and evaluating the opportunities for enhancing the human condition and the human organism opened up by the advancement of technology."[9] In other words, to transhumanists, the recent technological revolution marks the beginning of the end of the human species as we know it. In a very literal sense, they argue, we ought to see our new technologies as a bridge to what they call the "posthuman," a radically enhanced existence that far exceeds the imagination of contemporary brains. Central to the transhumanist vision of the posthuman is the prospect of "mind uploading," which will allegedly lead to a form of "digital immortality." Similar to the Spiritualist theory of the electronic afterlife world, the transhumanist idea is that the human brain, interpreted as a biological information processor, can essentially be digitally emulated, and that one's mind can subsequently be uploaded to a machine that replaces the biological hardware of the brain with a disembodied, synthetic one. Bostrom writes:

> A more radical kind of upgrade might be possible if we suppose a computational view of the mind. It may then be possible to upload a human mind to a computer, by replicating in silico the detailed computational processes that would normally take place in a particular human brain. Being an upload would have many potential advantages, such as the ability to make back-up copies of oneself (favorably impacting on one's life-expectancy) and the ability to transmit oneself as information at the speed of light.[10]

Wow—that sounds great! And some transhumanists believe that such mind-uploading technologies will become available already in the foreseeable future. An illustrative example is entrepreneur and author Martine Rothblatt's theory of "mindclones."[11] Mindclones, explains Rothblatt, "are mindfiles used and updated by mindware that has been set to be a functionally equivalent replica of one's mind." When a person cloned in such a fashion dies, their mindclone "will not feel that they have personally died, although the body will be missed in the same ways amputees miss their limbs but acclimate when given an artificial replacement." Some transhumanists argue that this kind of technologically enabled immortality will become not only possible but also cheap enough to be available to the masses. Philosopher Eric Steinhart, for example, foresees that in less than fifty years, so-called digital ghosts, which will be "both conscious and self-conscious," will inhabit the web by the millions, thus changing the online landscape beyond recognition.[12]

Rest assured—this is all nonsense. Despite the anthropomorphic term "artificial intelligence," the AI developed over the past couple of decades has very little, if anything, to do with human cognition or intelligence.[13] When we say that AI is becoming "smarter" or developing this or that cognitive ability, what we mean for the most part is not that it is becoming increasingly similar to a human brain but that we are becoming better and better at *decoupling* sophisticated tasks like natural language processing, or playing some board game, *from* intelligence. Many of the abilities that were previously thought to be the highest form of intelligence, like arithmetic and logic, have turned out to be easily replicated by even the dumbest machine, while creating a machine that understands even the most basic common sense is still hopelessly out of reach. Machines are not like people. So, whatever our data become after death, it is nothing like a "mindclone" or an artificial consciousness. Thrilling as it may be to discuss such prospects, it ultimately steals the light from more urgent issues. If all we do is run around assessing the implications of various sci-fi scenarios, there will not be any time for the real plausible scenarios that await us just around the corner. And this book is about the latter.

But surely, there must still be *some* kind of link between the deceased person and their animated data? Even if machines cannot make us immortal, digital technology clearly changes *something* about being dead, right? Indeed, it does, and here is where the metaphor of the *body* comes in handy. This metaphorical way of understanding personal data is often attributed to philosopher Luciano Floridi, whom I introduced in chapter 1, though he rarely uses it explicitly.[14] In simple terms, Floridi distinguishes between two ways of looking upon the status of personal data, of which he endorses the latter. The first approach, which is typically associated with the American tradition, sees personal data as something we *own*, like a car. If someone illicitly accesses my data, the violation can, from this perspective, be likened to either trespassing or theft. This comes with the advantage of situating data protection within property law, a particularly well-regulated area, which makes it easy to operationalize. (The German court ruling cited in the introduction of this chapter is a typical example of this approach.) The downside, as we shall see, is that it fails to capture central aspects of our relationship to information on both a metaphysical and an ethical level.

The other view, the one advocated by Floridi, is typically coupled with the European conception of privacy. It sees personal data as something constitutive of our personhood, something that we *are*, like a hand, rather than merely a possession. Let me elaborate, in case this does not sound immediately intuitive. If someone does something to your car, you may get upset and perhaps suffer financial loss, but ultimately, it will not affect who you are or whom you take yourself to be. What someone does to your data, by contrast, they do to *you*. For example, your biological being (i.e., your body) is literally constituted by the DNA in your cells, the genetic information that makes you, you. Those data *are* you, and they are you regardless of whether they are inscribed in proteins, on paper, or in computer code. When someone is dealing with your biometric data, that is, they are dealing with a piece of your body. Should they alter, manipulate, or disseminate those data, they are interfering with your (biological) being, violating the integrity of your informational body. The same goes for your social being. Data about your habits—how often you shower, what kinds of cosmetic products you use, whom you message with, what you click on—comprise information that constitutes who you are as a person. These are not merely data *about* an object that is you but informational shards that, when combined, *constitute* the thing that people refer to when speaking of the person that is you. They are parts of a larger narrative that helps you and others distinguish you from other people. The question "Who is X?" will always be answered by some unique sequence of information, whether in the format of genetic code or a narrative of actions through time. In other words, our bodies are best seen as consisting of information, and inversely, our information is best seen as analogous to our body—that is, as an *informational body*.

What does this have to do with the dead? Everything. Few, if any, metaphors better capture the status of digital remains than Floridi's informational body. For if we draw the metaphor one step further, we find that the data we leave behind upon death can be regarded as nothing less than an *informational corpse*. When we speak of digital remains, we should interpret the term literally as a form of human remains. The *corpus* of information left behind upon death is not just etymologically but also conceptually analogous to the corpse. No one has dissected the connection as meticulously as Australian philosopher Patrick Stokes.[15] Among the most important distinctions that Stokes brings to the fore is that between *selves* and *persons*. A *self*, according to Stokes, refers to the subjective experience of being a person—in other words, our consciousness. This part of who we are is completely terminated the moment the biological body breaks down. However convincing Eugina Kuyda's Roman bot becomes, there is no such thing as the experience of being a machine learning system, and in this sense, Roman is no more. A *person*, on the other hand, is the narrative *object* that we refer to when speaking of someone (including ourselves) in the third person, a body of information held together over time. Personal data, therefore, ought to be seen as a form of "digital flesh," and this part of who we are does not disappear at the moment of death but continues to live on *as long as our information prevails*. Indeed, as we saw in the previous chapter, personal information is often contained in spaces other than just the biological body—in other people's minds and memories, as well as through various forms of information technologies on which we engrave our being. So, whatever happens to our consciousness after death, *persons* clearly outlive their bodies.

This is why new information technologies so often become associated with the dead—they allow a bigger piece of the person to live on, further exposing the gap between the person and the self. Recall, for instance, Barthes's mediation on the nature of photography. When Barthes writes that photography is a "cunning dissociation of consciousness from identity," he is basically highlighting the same distinction as Stokes, only more poetically, and perhaps less formally. But the meaning is the same. Information technology dislocates the information that constitutes our person from the only hardware that can run a conscious subject—the biological body. The ontological status of digital remains of the dead is, in other words, to be regarded as analogous to the status of a biological body—an informational corpse, constitutive of a person, albeit not a self. And in this much, the transhumanists are right. Digital technologies *do* provide a form of immortality, or at least prolongation, of one's personhood, though whatever good comes from such a perpetuation of existence cannot be experienced because there is no subjective self there to experience it, only an informational corpse. Digital automation technologies and AI may reanimate it by making it talk, move, or even play a video game, but it inevitably remains a corpse. Nothing about it can "live forever" in any sense beyond the metaphorical.

Can the Dead Be Harmed?

Where does all this put us in terms of what we *should* do with the (digital) dead? One of the advantages of thinking about digital remains as a form of informational corpse is that it provides us with a culturally informed protocol for how to treat them properly. A dead body is not a mere possession of the bereaved. In almost all known cultures, it remains an entity entitled to its own, intrinsic value. When one person dies, it is the business of the entire community, indeed of the *human race as such* to ensure that it is properly laid to rest.

Unless they are complete monsters, even opposing armies let their enemies collect and care for their dead.

But this does not answer the more fundamental question of why it is *rational* to care for the bodies of the dead in the first place. The cultural fact that we *do* care is not the same as a justification for why we *should* care. Not all philosophers agree that we should, by the way. As early as the fourth-century BCE, philosopher Diogenes the Cynic argued that dead people (and their bodies) are beyond the realm of moral consideration. A man of his word, he even let it be known that, upon his death, he wished for his body to be tossed over the city walls to be devoured by wild beasts. When asked whether he would mind this foul treatment, he responded that he would not mind "as long as you provide me with a stick to chase the creatures away!" When confronted with the question of how he could possibly chase animals away when he was dead and hence lacked the awareness to control his body, he is supposed to have replied, "How am I then injured by being torn by those animals, if I have no sensation?"[16]

Some may dismiss Diogenes as more of a performer than a serious philosopher. He is, after all, known as the "dog philosopher." But the truth is that he was much respected in his day, and several more conventional philosophers have been inspired by his arguments. Epicurus, for instance, also argued that there was nothing to fear about death: "If I am, then death is not. If death is, then I am not. Why should I fear that which can only exist when I do not?"[17] Since both body and soul are material entities, he reasoned, the soul must be completely obliterated at the moment the body breaks down. Since neither soul nor (eventually) body exists after death, there is simply nothing to be harmed beyond this moment, since, according to Epicurus's hedonist ethics, "the good" must by definition be experienced by a conscious subject. Without a (material) subject to experience it, the good cannot be. Hence, neither the good nor its absence can befall the dead since they no longer exist.[18]

If we accept the above distinction between persons and selves, at least one part of the ancient philosophers' argument seems mistaken: Persons do survive the demise of the biological body insofar as they have been inscribed onto external objects. But is personhood a sufficient qualification to be a recipient of harm? Epicurus and Diogenes clearly did not think so, but many others have advanced arguments to show that it is. In this book, I am merely going to highlight one of them, namely, the English philosopher Thomas Nagel's notion of *facts of harm*.[19] For Nagel, some goods and evils are "irreducibly relational" in that we may understand them as *facts* rather than *states*. States of harm refer to things like pain, disappointment, depression, loss, and so on, basically ills that must be experienced to apply. Facts of harm, on the other hand, are bad regardless of whether they are experienced. For example, the fact that one has been betrayed is negative regardless of one's awareness of it, whereas the *state* of pain is negative only insofar as it is experienced. It is in a person's interests not to be conned or humiliated, whether they find out about it or not, because being respected is better than being disrespected. This, argues Nagel, implies that the fortunes and misfortunes of a person are not confined to the boundaries of his or her lifetime. For if the main argument for disregarding the moral status of the dead is their inability to have negative *experiences*, then any harm that applies regardless of one's experience must also apply to the dead. In fact, the boundaries of a lifetime are, according to Nagel, "commonly crossed by the misfortunes of being deceived, or despised, or betrayed." This explains what is wrong with, say, breaking a deathbed promise—it is "injury to the dead man" because it is the *fact* that he was betrayed, rather than the state of being betrayed (e.g., the emotional stress it causes), that is harmful.

I hold Nagel's distinction to be the strongest objection toward Epicurus's and Diogenes's hedonist argument.[20] Yet the concept of "facts of harm" is not especially useful in everyday life. It does not exactly connect the ethics of digital remains to some protocol from the tangible world. Hence, for our present discussion, I suggest we interpret Nagel's facts as violations of a dead person's right to be treated as a *person*. In other words, as violations of what is commonly referred to as *human dignity*. I concede that human dignity is a rather elusive concept. Its most common definition is derived from the ethics of Immanuel Kant, according to whom, all humans are members of what he calls "the kingdom of ends" by virtue of their capacity for autonomous moral reasoning (current, potential, or former). This means that humans are essentially ends in themselves, that cannot be measured, weighed, or matched with anything else. A person's dignity is, as Kant has it, "above all price," meaning that human beings must never be treated as *solely* a means to an end.[21] But this does not give much practical guidance.

Different cultures have different ideas about how a human ought to be treated. Book III of Herodotus contains an illustrative and commonly referenced episode. There it is told that when Darius was king of Persia, which was a truly multicultural empire, he summoned the local Hellenes to his court and asked them how much money they would demand in exchange for eating the dead bodies of their fathers, rather than cremating them. Naturally, the Hellenes responded that they would never do this, no matter how big the offered sum. Darius then summoned the cannibal tribe of Kallatiai and asked them their price to cremate their fathers' corpses instead of eating them. Like the Greeks, they responded in an outcry that they would never commit such a heinous crime, no matter what was on offer. In this narrative, both the Kallatiai and the Hellenes appeal to human dignity in their response to Darius, yet they draw opposite conclusions about how the dead should be treated. Still, our conclusion should not be that dignity is a useless concept, but that it is perhaps better understood as an *attitude* rather than a distinct practice. To be humiliated or degraded is an aggression to the dignity of a person (living or dead), a universal fact of harm, but what kind of treatment qualifies as humiliation is inevitably culturally contingent. The point is that, like the Hellenes and the Kallatiai, we possess preestablished cultural protocols to express this attitude.

As I argued in the beginning of this chapter, these protocols put us in a better position to deal with digital remains. For the entitlement to human dignity, I believe, offers an important critique of rulings like the case cited in the beginning of this chapter, where the decision to open a deceased person's private communications was justified explicitly by equating the girl's digital remains to (nonhuman) objects. To the court, her data were nothing but *means* by which the parents could find closure, possessions that can be inherited, bought, sold, and passed around without further ado. But as we have seen, such a view offers a mistaken, or in any case *insufficient*, understanding of what digital remains really are and why they are worthy of protection. It treats something that is essentially human as merely a thing, an estate that can be inherited and ultimately owned. It connects the intangible world of data to an inadequate tangible protocol. As soon as we think of digital remains as a body, however, this inadequacy comes to light. Bodies are certainly objects, and to some extent, it is reasonable to give those next to kin the final say in what is to happen to them after death, but they are not *just* objects. We do not *inherit* them, at least not in the sense of attaining ownership over them, like other possessions. Unlike estates, bodies remain under the protection of the law as objects constitutive of persons. The same sanctity, I hold, should be granted the informational body. I even hold that it would make sense to include them in international data protection legislation, such as the aforementioned GDPR in Europe. As such, the digital remains of the dead are not possessions that one ought to treat with a certain degree of dignity; they are constitutive of persons, who maintain an intrinsic right not to be treated as a mere means to an end.

According to Stokes, this status implies that preservation, rather than deletion, should be the default way of handling digital remains. Even if it is not perfectly intuitive, he has a strong case. The reason the boy racing his father in Rally Sports Challenge stops right before the finishing line is that winning would erase one of the few pieces that remain of the late father's agency. This is not just an act of self-interest. It is also, I believe, because the boy senses a moral imperative not to carelessly destroy the informational body of a deceased person. We do not simply erase the dead without further ado, because unlike other objects, they are not *just objects*, they are human objects—persons. I do not necessarily agree that existence is by default preferable to nonexistence. Just as one may kill out of respect (e.g., putting an injured animal out of its misery), one may similarly erase someone's data as a sign of respect—a kind of digital cremation, if you will. It all depends on the cultural manifestations of what is considered a proper way of dealing with a body. In the context of digital remains, we have no such cultural matrix to hold on to, so insofar as dignity goes, I am not sure either preservation or deletion has a stronger claim. For the biological body, however, we have hundreds of thousands of years of cultural development to help guide our expressions of respect and dignification. Connecting the two creates a conceptual bridge. It shows that the emergence of the informational corpse, futuristic as it may sound, is not a radical disruption. It is simply the continuation of a process that has been ongoing since we erected the first tombstones, namely, the separation between persons and biological bodies—or, better, the increasingly external nature of the informational body. We need to begin translating those rituals into the digital sphere.

The notion of the informational body is certainly not a universal tool for thinking about the ethics of posthumous data management. In some contexts it is immensely helpful, but in others it is only confusing. Part of the takeaway from this book is that digital remains are becoming a macro-level matter, and here, the comparison to bodies falls short. It may be useful to highlight the status of one person's digital remains, but when these accumulate by the billions, so that they encapsulate not merely persons but entire societies and generations, we cannot unpack the implications by analogy to digital mass graves or cemeteries. For this context, an entirely different sort of analogy is required.

The Digital Encyclopedia of the Dead

There is a short story by the Serbian author Danilo Kiš entitled "The Encyclopedia of the Dead."[22] It begins with a nameless woman traveling to Stockholm on invitation from a Mrs. Johansson at the Institute for Theatre Studies. One night, Mrs. Johansson takes the protagonist down to the archives of the Royal Library, where it has been arranged for her to freely explore the collection overnight. During this visit, the woman discovers a strange book entitled *The Encyclopedia of the Dead*, which turns out to comprise a complete record of every human life lived during the past three hundred years. Having recently lost her beloved father, she immediately begins searching for his entry. She finds it and is baffled by its comprehensiveness. Every detail of the old man's life, no matter how insignificant, has been recorded in the book. She reads about his childhood and adolescence, his time in the army, his travels, and his relationship to his family. She even learns about the motivations and subconscious forces that drove his strange behavior in the final days of his life. The book turns out to be more knowledgeable about the protagonist's father than she ever was, perhaps even than he ever was.

I was reminded of Kiš's short story as my colleague David Watson and I conducted a study that we, perhaps somewhat melodramatically, named "Are the Dead Taking Over Facebook? A Big Data Approach to the Future of Online Death."[23] By matching the age distribution of Facebook's user base in every country with projected life expectancy data from the United Nations, we predicted that by the end of this century, the platform will have accumulated over five billion profiles belonging to deceased users (see figure 1). Already by the mid-2050s, the number may surpass one billion, and by 2080, almost three billion. These calculations, however, were premised on a rather unlikely assumption, namely, that Facebook would continue growing at its current pace in all markets until saturation. Though the network's growth

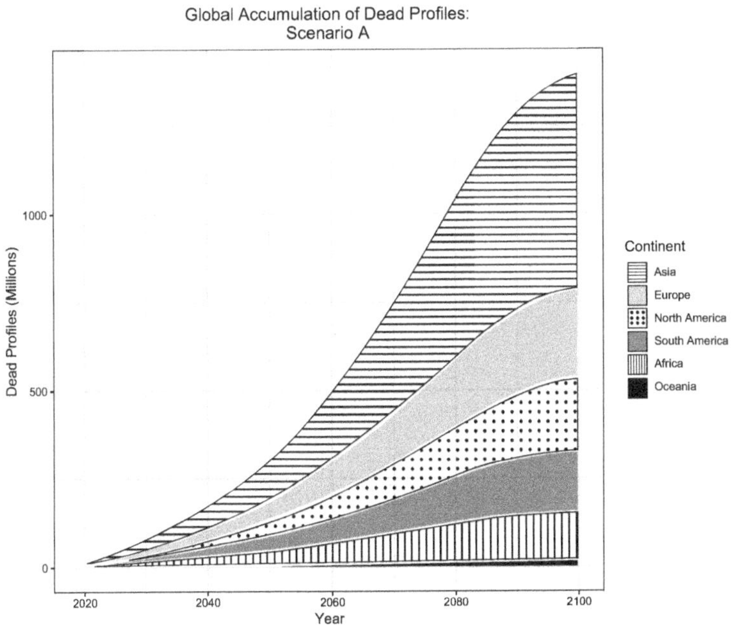

Figure 1. Geographic distribution of the expected accumulation of Facebook profiles of dead users, given continuous growth of the platform until market saturation.

remains strong, this is an unlikely scenario, so we made a second model, this time assuming that no new users would join from 2018 onward. This time, the total number of profiles of deceased users was "only" 1.4 billion by the century's end (see figure 2). However, the new assumption led to a distribution where already by the mid-2060s, there will be more profiles belonging to the deceased than to the living. It may even happen sooner than that, considering that the fastest-growing group on Facebook is users over sixty-five years old. In fact, a report from the Pew Research Center showed that in 2018 alone, that age group in the US rose from 22 to 40 percent in

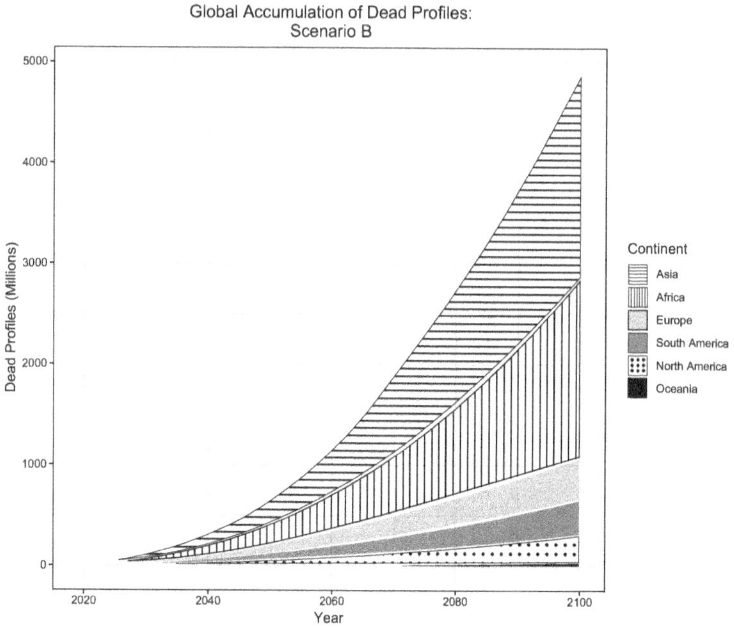

Figure 2. Geographic distribution of the expected accumulation of Facebook profiles of dead users, given no additional users after 2018

terms of Facebook penetration.[24] Melodramatic or not, the dead really do seem to be taking over Facebook.

The study made a big splash in the media. For weeks it seemed we did nothing but talk to journalists from around the world, explaining our method and warning about the consequences of our findings. There was undoubtedly a bit of sensationalism in the reporting. After all, Facebook becoming a digital cemetery makes a catchy headline. But for us, the important takeaway was not about Facebook specifically, for the same fate awaits any network that stores user data. We also tried our models on Instagram, for example, with very similar results.[25] Nor was it about which exact year the living population of some particular network will be surpassed by the dead. Such predictions are affected by way too many variables to be made with any serious precision. Instead, the big takeaway from our findings was that even under the most conservative assumptions, the number of deceased profiles on social media is growing exponentially, virtually encompassing an entire generation worldwide. In their effort to predict user behavior, and attract increasingly large audiences, the global tech giants are building a comprehensive record of almost every human on this planet, an archive which, just like in Kiš's fictional story, includes the inner, even subconscious thoughts and behavioral patterns of an entire generation. And these archives are slowly but surely turning into depositories of digital remains. They are, so to speak, becoming a *digital* encyclopedia of the dead.

Brutus's Closet

The sixteenth-century French philosopher Michel de Montaigne, known for his celebration of the particular and mundane over the spectacular and official elements of history, once wrote about Brutus:[26]

> I would rather choose to be certainly informed of the conference he had in his tent with some particular friends of his the night before a battle, than of the harangue he made the next day to his army; and of what he did in his closet and his chamber, than what he did in the public square and in the senate.[27]

Brutus belongs to the tiny minority of historical individuals about whom we actually know anything. Yet, unfortunately for Montaigne, what Brutus said to his comrades in his tent before battle will be forever lost, and so will pretty much everything else he ever did or said, apart from his official statements in the senate. Had he lived in the age of the internet, however, he would likely have spent the nights before his battles texting friends back in Rome, and those texts would have been part of an almost infinite network of interactions, an archive held by the app providing the service. The mere existence of such data, let alone their availability to historians, would surely have made Montaigne excited. And I imagine most contemporary historians would be keen to lay their hands on such an archive too. Imagine today, if researchers had access to Sir Winston Churchill's search history during the Second World War, to Napoleon Bonaparte's tweets, or to a YouTube clip of Jesus of Nazareth giving his Sermon of the Mount—or, better, what he did *after* the sermon, the things that Mathew does not mention and perhaps did not know about. The historical lessons would be invaluable, and for most of the events that will take place in the twenty-first century, something like this may actually be possible.[28]

Naturally, many historians have spoken in blissful terms of how the internet will revolutionize their trade.[29] Roy Rosenzweig, one of the first digital history pioneers, did, for instance, claim that due to the information people put on the internet, future historians will have access to an "essentially complete historical record."[30] Indeed, so-called big-data history is already becoming an established field thanks to our ever evolving capacity to produce and analyze large amounts of data.[31] Imagine what it will be in a hundred years' time. Like Kiš's protagonist gazing upon her father's entry in the encyclopedia, our descendants may, at least in theory, use our generation's aggregated digital footprints to zoom in on a given day and find out exactly what went on, who went where, who said what to whom, what people bought, clicked on, listened to, uploaded, and so on. Imagine, for instance, parsing through millions of tweets to analyze the response to a single trial like the prosecution of Kyle Rittenhouse, the teenager who traveled from Illinois to Wisconsin and fatally shot two people during the riots in the summer of 2020. Or analyzing the entire catalog of statements made by a single politician like Donald Trump, whose online presence has been more prolific than that of almost any other major political figure of the twenty-first century. Again, the value emerges from the *aggregation* of such data, which is why archives like Facebook, X (Twitter), and YouTube may become such significant resources for future generations. They allow broader inferences about entire populations and their reactions to various societal events over time. Rather than merely allowing an individual to study the life of their ancestor, the digital encyclopedia of the dead allows one generation to study the *society* of their predecessors. What if today, we could research the social patterns of communication that emerged in Germany in the 1930s, or track changes in sentiments toward the Reformation in Renaissance Europe? Again, the lessons learned would be invaluable. And this is why our digital data are something more than a mere collection of individual user histories; they are our collective past, part of humanity's digital heritage.

Unlike previous archives of human behavior, which are generally only focused on a subpopulation, the digital encyclopedia of the dead stretches over both geographic and demographic borders. Again, consider Facebook as an example. Contrary to how it is often described in popular and academic press, the emergence of the dead on the network is far from only a Western phenomenon. According my study with David Watson, European and North American users will actually represent a mere fraction of the users that are to leave profiles on the site in the next couple of decades. It is Asian countries that dominate, culminating with nearly 44 percent of the total by the end of the century (provided that Facebook's growth grinds to a halt). Moreover, in the scenario where Facebook continues growing, African nations will make up the second-largest share of the platform's historical record. Nigeria in particular becomes a major hub of Facebook user deaths—in fact, the second largest in the world, after India—accounting for over 6 percent of the global total. Niger, Mali, and Burkina Faso also appear in the top ten countries by dead profile count, while the United States is the only Western nation to even crack the list. Facebook's future archives of digital remains are, in other words, a truly global archive of human behavior.[32] The same goes for most of the tech empires that dominate the digital economy. YouTube, for instance, has localized versions in more than one hundred countries and is the most commonly used social media platform in many of the world's key markets, including Brazil, the Philippines, and Indonesia.[33] More than five hundred hours of video material are uploaded to its servers every minute. TikTok connects roughly one in every five internet users in the world (one in three in Asia), and that number is probably way higher among younger demographics, as 41 percent of TikTok's user base is between the ages of sixteen and twenty-four. I could go on, but the bottom line is this: The data archives harbored by these platforms are more than an advertising resource; they are a global portrait of our species in the twenty-first century.

The archives of the social web also comprise a much higher demographic diversity than previous records. To date, our knowledge of the past and its inhabitants has been highly skewed. We may know a lot about kings, generals, and politicians like our dear Brutus—the elites who dominated the societies of the past—yet almost nothing is known about the ordinary people who inhabited those societies. For instance, compared to people like Brutus, we know virtually nothing about the hundreds of thousands of enslaved individuals who populated ancient Rome. How did they live? What were their lives, dreams, desires like? We will never know. Most striking is the absence of named women in history. According to English historian Bettany Hughes, women account for only 0.5 percent of the historical individuals whose names we know, despite representing 50 percent of our ancestors.[34] Then again, the women of history whom we actually do know something about do not receive nearly the attention they deserve. But that is a different matter. The point here is that most women, along with several other marginalized or economically disadvantaged groups, were never allowed into our records in the first place.

But this is now potentially changing. Not in the sense that decisions on how and whom to record are made democratically, but in the sense that in the digital realm, recording, not forgetting, has become the default.[35] When something happens, it is the rule, rather than the exception, that it leaves some kind of record behind. As such, the information society reverses the logic of previous record writing; instead of asking "Is this important enough to record?" we now ask "Is this record *unimportant* enough to destroy?" For most people and events of the twenty-first century, a record already exists; the question is only what makes it worth keeping. So, for the first time in the history of our species, we now have a data record that is truly reflective of human diversity, at least for the part of the population that is online (even though, as we shall see, this is far from everyone). The vision for a diverse and reflective history is, for the first time ever, a realistic possibility, and if it is spoiled, it will be because someone's data are *intentionally* destroyed.

Of course, none of this requires that the data studied are digital remains.[36] To some degree, research on contemporary users is already being done internally by many platforms, mainly for the purpose of figuring out how to make users buy more things or to increase their time spent on the platform, but also for genuinely good causes like suicide prevention.[37] Sharing all that data with the public, so that other researchers can utilize it, would have the potential to do a lot of good and make significant improvements in our understanding of society. Meanwhile, data sharing also opens up a massive potential for harming the individuals who are being analyzed. In 2006, Harvard researchers began scraping the Facebook profiles of Harvard's class of 2009, which they matched with information about students' majors and residences. The published study, known as "Tastes, Ties, and Time," made some valuable insights into how social networks and friendships form over time.[38] But, despite the researchers' efforts to "anonymize" the data, and their replacing of Harvard with "a diverse private college in the Northeastern U.S.," it took only days before people figured out the real identity of the school and hence also those of the students. In the end the study probably contributed to Facebook's decision to essentially close the platform for research collaborations a couple of years later. The point is that while big data research on living subjects may be valuable, it poses a threat not only to the dignity but also to the well-being of its subjects. Historical research, by contrast, does not pose a risk to well-being, that is, the *states of harm* that it might cause its subjects—because they are dead. Unlike scraping the profiles of current Harvard students, reading the diaries of, say, the students of Plato's academy does not change those students' prospects in life.

But hang on a moment. Using digital remains as a means to gain historical insight—is this not exactly the type of violation of human dignity of the dead that I discussed in the first half of this chapter? Possibly. Doing research on the private communications of individuals from the past may well constitute a harm to their dignity, at least insofar as it treats them *only* as a means to an end. But my larger point here is not that future generations *should* do research on the private communications of each of us. It is that they may have an interest in doing it on some of us and that it matters greatly who ends up controlling this activity (i.e., who owns the data and their motives for using it). This (potential) conflict of interest between and within generations is a major point that I shall get back to toward the end of the book. But for now, let us merely state that when we zoom out and think about digital remains in the aggregate, they emerge not merely as a private concern for individual users and bereaved families but as an informational heritage, an encyclopedia of the dead, passed down from one generation to the next. This is why the accumulation of digital remains on the web is a collective matter, a concern even for those who do not know a single person who has died and left data online. Digital remains are a matter of our *collective* (digital) past, and insofar as we care about future generations and their relationship to the past, we should care about what happens to the digital remains of our generation.

Because of the global scope and unprecedented diversity of the encyclopedias of the social web, I believe that they hold what British Ghanaian philosopher Kwame Anthony Appiah calls a *cosmopolitan value*, that is, a value that goes beyond the interests of any single individual or community.[39] Let me elaborate.

A typical example of an artifact with cosmopolitan value is the Great Pyramids of Egypt. Naturally, these monuments are an important national heritage of everyone living in Egypt. But they do not belong exclusively to the Egyptians, for the wonder of the Great Pyramids is not only part of Egyptian history but part of the history of all humankind. There are de facto no pharaonic Egyptians left, and so the remains of ancient Egypt are of little more cultural significance to the the predominately Muslim population of today's Egypt than to the billions of people worldwide who rightly see themselves as cultural descendants of ancient Egypt. The preservation and integrity of the Great Pyramids are concerns for all members of humanity, because these artifacts tell us something about who we are and from whence we came. They belong to all of us. As Appiah stresses, though, the word *belong* has an entirely metaphoric meaning here. The Pyramids remain the property not of the UN or any other organization working in the name of "humanity" but of the Egyptian state, and rightly so. Yet, this does not mean that the state of Egypt can do whatever it wants with the remains of the ancient empire, for their *cosmopolitan value* comes with duties to the species of whose history they are part. Like corpses and other objects constitutive of the dead, the Pyramids are not "just objects."

As we increasingly live our lives online, it is only natural that digital artifacts too will come to hold such a status. It may seem silly today, but the data records we are building through our everyday online activities are de facto the largest archives of human behavior ever assembled in the history of our species. Just as the Pyramids tell the story of early human civilization, these data tell something about human civilization at the cusp of the twenty-first century, about the birth of digital society. They are, or will at least become, part of our *digital world heritage*.

Several initiatives are already taking form to preserve the social web for posterity. Examples range from temporary projects such as the pioneering Task Force on Archiving of Digital Information, to international organizations such as the Digital Preservation Coalition and UNESCO's Software Heritage Project (the latter has the ambitious mission to preserve *all* open-source software in the world for posterity!).[40] The most widely known among these is probably the Internet Archive, an organization that has been ambitiously working since 1996 to provide "universal access to all knowledge." It is best known to the public for the Wayback Machine, a publicly accessible and searchable online archive that contains old versions of (most) open pages on the World Wide Web. Meanwhile, national archives in several countries are working to preserve tweets and other social media content from political leaders and notable public figures who are deemed to have cultural significance. The Library of Congress in the United States, for example, has gathered material from the web for over two decades with the aim to build an archive representative of American web history for future scholars. It has currently amassed more than eighteen billion digital documents comprising a total of 2.129 petabytes of data, and in 2010, Twitter announced that it would donate its entire archive to the library. Though the plans to make the archive searchable and accessible to the public are yet to be realized, the sheer ambition is an indicator of how social media data are increasingly viewed as historically significant.[41]

These initiatives are certainly on the right path, but for reasons that I explore in more detail in chapter 4, they suffer from some serious insufficiencies, at least in comparison to the *real* archives held by the tech giants. The fact that national archives and nongovernmental organizations gather tweets from politicians and other notable media personalities is great, but as historical resources, these data are but a drop in the ocean of the data harbored by Big Tech. They may capture what our modern-day Brutuses say in the senate, but what he does in his closet, the greater patterns of his followers' reactions, and the power that comes with this information, belong exclusively to the handful of firms that currently own the encyclopedias of the dead.

Not So Valuable After All?

There are several possible counterarguments to the claim that social data are a valuable historical resource. Many readers have probably thought of some of them already, so I better address them right away before moving on.

The most common objection is that social media data tell very little about our "real" lives, that they are mundane "trash" and therefore lack the significance of other, more dignified, documents such as government records. It is simply not of interest to future generations, it is said, to know what someone ate for breakfast on a particular day in the beginning of the twenty-first century, nor how cute their cat was—not to speak of the avalanche of memes that have been shared in the past ten years. Are not such data too mundane to be of any interest to posterity? I acknowledge that, figuratively speaking, much of what is on social media may well be akin to trash—but this does not make it worthless. On the contrary, archaeologists often find trash piles and sewers to be among the richest resources for scientific insight about the past. "Trash is a proxy for human behavior," to quote Harvard anthropologist Richard Meadow.[42] In fact, much of what archaeologists have learned about the lives of past humans comes from those humans' trash.[43] Temples and monuments may tell us about the elites and extremes of ancient civilizations, yet they disclose little about the everyday lives of the ordinary people who inhabited them. That which people consider mundane, by contrast, is often rich with information about what they take for granted—that is, their day-to-day lives. So if social media data appear like "trash" to us now, it does not mean that they will remain trash to future generations. Rather, precisely because we do consider them mundane, our most trivial memes and breakfast meal posts may in fact become significant for those who come after.

A second line of critique holds that social media provide an unreliable representation of reality. Online self-portrayal, some say, presents a polished and ultimately false image of what goes on in "real life." If some alien civilization studied humanity in the twenty-first century only through what we post on, say, Instagram, they would probably think life here was all about beautiful sunsets, fitness influencers, and cute animals, and we all know that is not quite accurate. There is a great deal of important activity that never makes it to social media, and what does is often heavily manipulated to be more appealing.

I have two responses to this criticism. First, while I contend that one's online self-portrayal necessarily provides only a selective and curated image, it may still be valuable for scientific purposes. How people wish to be perceived is just as important as the hard facts about their lives, and it is often by comparing the living conditions of a population with its self-image that we come to learn deep truths about cultural values and trends. The fact that a person or group who posts only about their cute pets is at the same time suffering great economic despair tells you something about them that the economic data alone could not. Hence, however manipulated they may be, social media posts are real actions that tell something about a social reality. Second, and more crucial, I believe it is a mistake to view social media data as merely a representation of what goes on in some supposedly "real" world. On the contrary, society is increasingly taking place *within* online social networks. As Floridi's concept of the "onlife" illustrates, life is never purely on- or offline but always takes place in a network of connected technologies and people.[44] For example, many historically significant events and movements, such as #MeToo and to some extent even the Arab Spring, were not merely representations of events taking place "in real life" but were, from the very beginning, digital movements. The data and the events are one. The objection that one does not reflect the other does not make sense.

The third, and certainly most poignant, objection to my claim that social media data are valuable is that not all of today's society takes place online. Although twenty-first-century life to a large degree is and will be characterized by the onlife experience, this mode of being is by no means universally shared. According to Internetwordstats.com, 40 percent of the world's population is not connected to the internet. This statistic is high even in some developed countries, such as Greece, where more than 17 percent of the population lacks access.[45] Whereas this number will likely decrease rapidly in the coming decade, there is still evidence to suggest that access alone is not sufficient to make people use the internet. In the UK, for example, which has an internet penetration rate of about 95 percent, roughly one in every ten persons lacks even basic skills in using it.[46] When we speak of the historical value of social media data, it is therefore important to avoid illusions of a "complete" record of all corners of society, at least until all digital divides are bridged. But even then, digital history should not be equated with "the past." As we shall see in the following chapter, data are always collected and organized for a specific purpose, and that purpose, whatever it may be, will be reflected in the data.

In addition to these objections, one may add a final one: namely, that it is extremely implausible that the tech industry's data will ever be shared with researchers, even in a hundred years' time. How do we even know that Facebook and Google, or something like them, will exist long enough to become a *historical* resource? And if they do, how likely is it that they will share their archives with researchers outside the company? Is it even desirable that the industry would share dead people's data, presumably without their consent, for historical research? These are all valid questions. And yes, it is conceivable that future generations will never be able to harness the power of the digital encyclopedias of the dead. But this is not my point. My point is that the data harbored by the tech industry holds *the potential* to massively improve humanity's future understanding of the past and its inhabitants. Furthermore, even if it may never come to the benefit of the public, someone, most likely the firms that dominate the industry today, *will* possess this power. They will, in a rather literal way, own our (digital) past. And they *will* do research on that data, whether you like it or not. In aggregation, our digital remains are de facto the remains of an entire generation. Whether this awesome archive will be kept intact and who will be able to use it are questions for the remainder of this book. For now, what matters is that thinking of our aggregated digital remains as a single artifact, as a digital encyclopedia of the dead, reveals the collective nature of the phenomenon. What happens to your data when you die is not merely some private concern for you and those close to you; we all have a stake in what happens to the encyclopedias inscribed to the servers of Big Tech.

* * *

The metaphors of the body and the encyclopedia do not exclude other understandings of the dead—we may just as well talk about digital estates, ghosts, souls, or the undead. But they are crucial tools to make sense of the post-mortal condition in that they link its nascency to pre-digital objects that are already familiar to us, and the cultural protocols that come with them. They allow us to formulate more specific questions and, thus, to better understand the challenges posed by the post-mortal condition. If someone's digital remains are constitutive of a person entitled to human dignity, how should we understand the increasing commodification of such materials? What happens when the digital encyclopedia runs out of (metaphorical) pages for new names? Who owns it? And is not the encyclopedia also full of living people sharing those pages? Now that our basic metaphoric vocabulary is in place, I shall begin answering these questions.

3 * The Rise of the Digital Afterlife Industry

> Capital is dead labour, which, vampire-like, lives only by sucking living labour, and lives the more, the more labour it sucks.
>
> **Karl Marx**

Ash & Martha

In "Be Right Back," the opening episode of the TV show *Black Mirror*'s second season, the protagonist, Martha, loses her partner Ash in a car accident.[1] Martha is devastated. But right after the funeral, she receives an invitation to try a beta version of a new app. The hook is as intriguing as it is uncanny: Using a recently deceased person's digital footprint as its basis—their search data, conversation logs, tweets, snaps, playlists, and so on—the app analyzes the patterns and produces a chatbot that is a hyperrealistic replica of the personality of the deceased. Martha is at first skeptical, even insulted, by the mere suggestion. Ash is dead, and no algorithm in the world can change that. But then she makes a shattering discovery—she is pregnant with Ash's child. After a few hours of agony, she can no longer hold off. She must speak to Ash. She decides to use the service in order to send no more than one message to the chatbot replica: "I am pregnant." But it is far from the last message she sends.

Due to Ash's frequent usage of his electronic devices, the chatbot replica turns out to be stunningly accurate. It has the same humor (even better!), the same timing, and the same jargon as the original. For a person like Martha, whose life and sense of self is in shambles, it proves an invaluable comfort in coping with her newly discovered pregnancy. She continues the chat with Ash's digital ghost, and after some time communicating with it, she writes, "I wish we could talk." The bot responds, "What if we could?" As it turns out, the app also offers a premium version, which includes a voice service. Using recordings of Ash's voice from old clips and videos, the app is able to replicate the sound of his voice, which means that Martha is now able to call the chatbot anytime she feels the need to, which soon becomes pretty much *all the time*. Eventually, Martha takes the final step toward resurrecting Ash and orders a complete humanoid robot programmed to move and behave like Ash. As you may have guessed, the robot is not quite like Ash (despite some of his features arguably being improved), and the story does not have an entirely happy ending. In the end, Robot Ash is locked in the attic, presumably a secret from the outside world.

"Be Right Back" asks difficult questions about life, death, and mourning. With what authority does Martha "resurrect" her late spouse? Is it good for her? And what is the ethical status of the robot? Unsurprisingly, the episode has become a frequent point of reference in debates over digital remains. Yet one crucial detail of the story tends to be overlooked in these debates, namely, the anonymous firm that provides the technology. Though Martha's perpetuation of her relationship with Ash is technologically mediated, the technology does not arise in and of itself. It is designed by someone, and for a particular purpose. The episode offers only limited information about who they are and what their motives may be. But, at least if as the firm is anything like real-life businesses, its purpose is presumably to make money. Indeed, this seems to be Ash's prime function from the firm's point of view. In each of the instances when Martha chooses to upgrade, the option is first introduced by the bot itself. For instance, it is "Ash's" texts that promote the voice service when Martha mentions her wish that they could talk. And if the bot is really an incarnation of Ash, who is she to deny her late husband, whom she loves above everyone else? In other words, Robot Ash is at the same time a product provided by a firm *and* the perfect salesman for that product. He is not programmed to be just like Ash, but—at least insofar as the company has been successful in its goal—to be the version of him that Martha is most likely to continue paying for.

As we shall see, this commercial angle puts not only the episode but the entire digital afterlife phenomenon in a new light. For it is not only in fiction that our interactions with the online dead are mediated by commercial platforms. Indeed, in the real world, for-profit logic is the rule rather than the exception. But what are the consequences of such commercialism? How is it shaping our relationship to the dead, and what are the ethical implications?

The Digital Afterlife Industry

To my knowledge, there is yet no service with the technological sophistication depicted in "Be Right Back." But reality is not far behind. In 2015, MIT start-up Eterni.me launched a beta version of a chatbot—including a virtual avatar—which, it claimed, would let you "Skype with the dead." Provided a sufficient amount of data, the algorithms would be able to extract one's personality and turn it into an interactive avatar.[2] It reached forty-seven thousand subscribers before the site mysteriously went down in 2021, possibly due to running out of seed funding. But similar apps keep emerging. The most recent is Hereafter AI, which offers the same product as Eterni.me, though mainly based on interviews with the person to be replicated. It appears that this app is having relative market success. However, the most successful, though perhaps less clear-cut, case of this type of service is Replika, a for-profit app founded by Eugenia Kuyda, whom I introduced in the previous chapter. The product has developed significantly since the simplicity of the Roman bot, but the basics follow roughly the same logic: You train a chatbot by interacting with it and by giving it access to your data, and eventually it becomes more and more like you—an artificial best friend who is also a version of yourself. There are several similar start-ups, but with over ten million users, Replika is by far the most successful, perhaps partly thanks to the toning-down of the afterlife angle in their brand.[3]

Though it remains mainly a start-up phenomenon, the quest to make "Be Right Back" reality is also on the agenda of the tech giants. In June 2022, Rohit Prasad, senior vice president of Amazon and head scientist of its virtual assistant software Alexa, announced that the company had developed a feature that enabled Alexa to speak in the voice of a deceased relative. Amazon even made a promotional video for it, in which a young boy asks Alexa to read *The Wizard of Oz* in the voice of his departed grandmother. Similar applications have been available for quite some time. In 2017, an Irish start-up used a deep-learning algorithm to analyze voice recordings of US President John F. Kennedy and created a synthetic replicant voice, which they made read the speech he was about to give on November 22, 1963, when he was assassinated in Dallas. It sounds just like the real thing. But such precedents have required enormous amounts of data, whereas Alexa needs only one minute of recorded voice data to successfully replicate a person's voice, meaning that the new feature will become available to a much broader market.

Just a year before the announcement of Alexa's ability to replicate voices, Microsoft got a patent for a similar technology, only in this case it creates a replica of an entire personality, not just a voice. The patent document explains:

> The specific person [whom the bot represents] may correspond to a past or present entity (or a version thereof), such as a friend, a relative, an acquaintance, a celebrity, a fictional character, a historical figure, a random entity, etc. The specific person may also correspond to oneself (e.g., the user creating/training the chat bot).[4]

Though Microsoft officials have denied the intention of developing a product for the market, the patent does undeniably sound very much like a real-life version of *Black Mirror*, following in the footsteps of multiple start-ups that emerged during the 2010s.

It remains to be seen whether the demand for posthumous chatbots will increase. The current record does not make the future of this technology look too bright, considering the fate of, for example, Eterni.me, and the fact that the mere thought of communicating with a dead person through their data still strikes most people as a bit creepy. Yet perhaps, as we become increasingly accustomed to interacting with chatbots in everyday life, chatting with a deceased loved one will feel just as normal as looking at a picture of them. In any case, the industry is clearly gearing up already.

The chatbot services understandably attract a lot of attention in popular media. Yet the vast majority of services that seek to monetize digital remains do not use AI. In fact, the first ones had emerged already in the late 1990s, long before the big AI boom of the past decade. These were rudimentary services like Finalthoughts.com, founded by internet entrepreneur Michael Krim. Krim conceived of the idea in 1999 during an unusually unpleasant flight involving some serious turbulence. While in the air, certain of his approaching demise, he began thinking of what he would have said to his loved ones if he had had the chance. Fortunately, the plane landed safely, but the episode inspired Krim to found what would become the world's first *online posthumous messaging service*. Rather than an AI predicting what a user *would have said* were they alive (this concept still belonged to the world of sci-fi in the '90s), Finalthoughts.com used authentic messages written by living users that would dispatch to a series of designated email addresses in the event of the users' deaths. The service itself did not live long, though. In 2004 it had already gone out of business.

Nevertheless, a plethora of similar services would soon emerge, many offering more sophisticated versions of the same product. Most firms still offered merely the dispatch of an email or other forms of text-based message. Others, like the Israeli start-up SafeBeyond, offered considerably more versatile services, ranging from personalized videos to messages dispatched on given dates, such as the future birthdays of a user's children. (This last function is suggestive of rap artist Kanye West's hologram resurrection of his late father-in-law for his now-ex-wife Kim Kardashian's birthday.) The promotional video displayed on the SafeBeyond landing page, for instance, features a wedding at which each family member receives a video greeting from the bride's departed father. The son is instructed to watch over the family, the daughter is ensured how proud her late father is of her, and so on.

Some services have focused instead on perpetuating their users' social media presence. The innovative but short-lived start-up Liveson, for instance, promised to continue posting automated tweets from its users' Twitter profiles after their deaths, using the catchy slogan "When your heart stops beating, you'll keep tweeting." All in all, posthumous messaging services have had varying success. Some have remained as a tiny niche market. Others, like the Islamic prayer apps discussed in chapter 2, are fundamentally changing the way the dead remain visible online.

Many of the early digital afterlife services were also digital security vaults that helped users deal with problems of digital asset management that may arise following their own or someone else's departure—including deposits of passwords, digital collections, video game avatars, subscriptions to steaming sites, and so on. An oft-cited pioneer of such services is Legacy Locker, founded by entrepreneur Jeremy Toeman. A couple of years prior to founding Legacy Locker, Toeman had struggled (and failed) to access his departed grandmother's Hotmail account. Then—coincidentally also during an unpleasant flight—he realized that his own digital legacy would be far messier to clean up than his grandmother's. In a 2011 interview with the Bay Area's *Mercury News*, Toeman explains:

> I'm on a plane to New York, and it's really bumpy, and I'm thinking, hmm, what would happen if . . . ? And I realized that of all the things I'd properly accounted for through my estate plan and trust, the one thing that wasn't accounted for were

> my Web domains. I own 100 or so, and they could have value if auctioned off after my death, but my wife would never be able to find out about them. That was it. I thought, this could be a business.[5]

It really could be a business. After the launch of Legacy Locker, several other start-ups, such as Entrust and DataInherit (both of which now belong to SecureSafe), followed suit with similar *information management services*. The idea was to provide a form of digital will that ensured that assets would be passed on to their appropriate heirs (or destroyed). Several firms even started collaborations with life insurance companies and funeral homes to make sure the consumer's afterlife was as easily manageable for the bereaved as possible, both on- and offline. Eventually, bigger firms implemented similar features, like Google's Inactive Account Manager, which lets users appoint a "trusted contact" who will be able to download parts of the user's data in the event of their death. While Inactive Account Manager effectively solved many of the problems addressed by the start-up scene, information management services remain popular to this day. In any case, I regularly receive requests from similar start-ups firms asking for endorsements or ethical counseling.

By far the most common form of digital afterlife service, however, is the *online memorial*. These are sites and apps that often look like social media platforms on the surface, only the pages/profiles are not meant for the living but for the dead. Unlike a physical site, like a cemetery, the online memorial site can gather geographically and temporally dispersed communities to come together to mourn, either by uploading their own material (e.g., photos, videos) or by leaving messages for the deceased. Online memorials come in all kinds of niches. Some sites specialize in accommodating deceased children.[6] Some focus on fallen veterans. Some are even devoted to beloved pets.[7] In 2007, Facebook launched a so-called memorialization feature that gave bereaved families the right to either delete or memorialize a profile of a person who they could prove had passed away (typically by submitting a death certificate or obituary). If they opted for the latter, the profile would remain on the network, albeit with some modifications. The text "Remembering" would be added before the deceased person's name, and the profile would be closed off from the search function, unable to receive friend requests, and free of ads. It would also be removed from birthday reminders and the "people you may know" feature. In 2015, a feature called "legacy contact" was added on top of this, which let users appoint another Facebook user to be the custodian of their profile in the event of their death. The custodian does not get access to the entire memorialized account but is able to moderate posts on the timeline, change profile photos, write posts to the mourning community, and so on. These features were then even further developed in 2019, with tribute pages separated from the original timelines of deceased users, and an AI function that "detected" supposed deaths in order to proactively remove profiles from appearing in inappropriate places, such as lists of "people you may know." It almost goes without saying that Facebook implementing these features essentially rendered many of the start-up services redundant. Why upload a bunch of old photos and videos of a deceased loved one, which you may struggle to get access to on a new, unreliable site, when everything you need is already set up automatically on Facebook? Moreover, if the deceased individual has chosen a legacy contact, that person will even get a notification with an invitation to create a memorial upon that person's departure. It is all set up and ready to go. Given these massive benefits, the future of memorials is probably on Facebook or some large, stable behemoth like it.

Despite their differences, the various types of firms accounted for above all share a single trait: in one way or another, they seek to monetize some aspect of people's digital afterlife. Collectively, we may refer to them as the *digital afterlife industry* (DAI), an umbrella term that includes virtually any commercial enterprise that makes digital remains part of its business plan.[8]

Most DAI businesses have names that relate to perpetuity, such as B-emortal, Eterniam, Eterni.me, Eter9, InfiBond, Perpetu, SafeBeyond, and so on. Ironically, this has not stopped most of them from going out of business only a few years after their launches. In 2017, I published a study mapping out the various branches of the industry, which included a list of fifty-eight different firms.[9] Only a handful remain active today. Despite their ambitious names, neither SafeBeyond, Eterni.me, B-emortal, nor Perpetu could survive without money. Perhaps making a business out of digital remains is not so lucrative after all. Or the market just was not mature when these pioneering businesses launched, the population of the internet still too young to be thinking about their potential demise. In a few years, when interacting with chatbots may feel just as normal as paying with a credit card, and the mean age of the internet's population approaches that of the population in general, the market will perhaps be ready even for the boldest businesses like Eterni .me and Replika. We can only wait and see, but considering the steady stream of new start-ups joining the industry, it is not a wild guess.

Another explanation of why many of the early digital afterlife services failed is the entry of Facebook and Google into the market. In 2010, a start-up that let you choose whom your emails would be passed down to upon death offered a unique product. The same was true for memorial sites that let friends and family come to mourn a deceased person and share pictures and other (digital) memories of them. Since then, such features have become mainstream. As I mentioned, Google's Inactive Account Manager lets users do precisely what so many start-ups set out to do, and Facebook has implemented a variety of death-related features, from memorialization of profiles to the legacy contact, which draw on the innovations that initially emerged within the start-up scene.[10] It is impossible to say how many people actively use the death-related features offered by Google and Facebook, but I would personally be shocked by anything short of a hundred million, given that Facebook claims thirty million people view memorialized profiles every month. Does this mean that the tech giants are now part of the DAI? The answer is no and yes. Take Facebook as an example. On the one hand, death and the dead were certainly not on top of Mark Zuckerberg's mind when he created the network back in 2004. The site was even criticized in its early days for not properly accommodating mourners.[11] Moreover, when Facebook eventually launched its memorialization feature, thus making interaction with the dead part of the platform, it intentionally *de*commercialized the memorialized profiles. That is, unlike the rest of Facebook, memorialized profiles do not display any advertisements. When visiting a memorialized profile, you will not be bombarded with ads for funeral homes, counselors, and flower shops. So, since the posthumous interaction on Facebook is explicitly noncommercial, it does not really make sense to include it in the DAI—insofar as it deals with digital remains, it is only doing so involuntarily.

On the other hand, the commercial aspects may be unavoidable. Even if the profit deriving from the traffic to the memorialized profiles themselves is negligible so far, the long-term effects of hosting these profiles may prove advantageous. Insofar as users value and care for the digital presence of the dead, they will also care for the continuation of the privately owned platforms where the dead reside. When, in 2020, Twitter announced its plans to remove profiles that had been inactive for more than six months, it was met with fierce user outrage. Tech journalist Drew Orlanoff wrote in a *TechCrunch* article, fearing the loss of his late father's tweets: "My heart sank. And I cried. You see, I didn't think about this. It is a big deal. [. . .] Think about it, Twitter. Do better."[12] He surely was not alone. Bereaved parents have been observed attending (and communicating with) the digital remains of their deceased children for years after their death. Many even hold such ongoing communication as a moral imperative. "We do it to keep him alive," said one of the interviewees of a study led by sociologist Jo Bell.[13] So Twitter ultimately had to reverse its decision. The lesson here is that these protests were testaments to a sense of *belonging*, and such a sentiment may hold great commercial potential.[14] It provides social media companies a rare opportunity to consolidate their inevitability for society, essentially appropriating the role churches used to play in Western Christian culture. Cemeteries may not in themselves be society's most lucrative businesses, but they have unique capacity to forge bonds between people and the soil in which their departed loved ones lie buried. When this "soil" is a for-profit online platform rather than a geographical space, that bond may prove highly profitable.

People will stay on Facebook, or at least continue to care for its existence, because it is where their loved ones, living or dead, are to be found.

It is unlikely that Facebook's memorialization feature is part of some elaborate plan with the intention to appropriate central cultural functions in society. But the takeaway here is not that the tech giants have some hidden agenda in their appropriation of features from the DAI start-up scene. It is that every business that stores its users' personal data will eventually, whether it intends to or not, become stewards of their digital remains. This could be seen as a burden, in that the digital remains may need to be destroyed, which may turn out to be rather costly.[15] But it could also be turned into a rare opportunity to become even more intertwined with the social fabric of society. Make no mistake, any rational for-profit firm will choose the latter. And this is why the monetization of the online dead is related to *you*, even if you are not planning on subscribing to a posthumous chatbot service and have no intention of using online memorials. Insofar as you use the internet, you are leaving some trail of information behind, especially if you are using social media. Indeed, even the most passive user produces a ton of information every time they log in. And when you die, these data will still be there, stewarded under the same logic that governs all businesses—the logic of profit.

Critiquing the Industry

Many people feel an intuitive unease about making a business out of our relationship to the dead. Indeed, controversies over mixing death and business go a long way back.[16] Though this instinct may be justified, it is no justification in and of itself. If something is morally questionable, one must ensure that the explanation of *why* and *how* it is questionable makes sense before doing anything about it. In the case of the DAI, this means that any ethical review of the industry must be grounded in a systematic critique, rather than some casual gut feeling.

Let us begin crafting such a critique by examining the economics of the industry, that is, *how* it makes money out of digital remains. First, we should note that the DAI comprises different modes of monetization. Some firms use a "freemium" model, where the basic service is free but in-app purchases unlock more functions (SafeBeyond used this model). Some, like GoodTrust, offer more traditional subscriptions for consumers to purchase. Others use a "free of charge" model, where the primary commodity is not the site consumed by the users but, rather, the surplus attention they generate in doing so, which can be sold as targeted advertising to third parties (Facebook would arguably fall within this category). Here, it is the mourners who assume the role of the labor force, performing a form of *audience labor*, as proposed by critical theorist Christian Fuchs.[17] The value arises not out of the work put down by those who maintain and design the platforms but by the masses who use them. The bigger the audience the bigger the advertising space, which is essentially what most platforms make money from. As such, the firms depend on what Swedish sociologist Magdalena Kania-Lundholm calls "digital mourning labor."[18] The dead become a means to be worked by a labor force of mourners for the end of profit.[19]

Irrespective of these various modes of monetization, the goal of each DAI firm is to increase traffic to its site, and this requires some form of investment—for example, a workforce to administer the traffic, a platform where interaction can take place, and, of course, server space where the digital remains can be stored. Only if the traffic (the interaction with digital remains) generates a monetary value that exceeds this investment will the firm survive. Given that it does, however, the profit will need to be reinvested in even more server space and so forth, in order to keep up with the growth of competitors. For illustration, assume that a company harbors one million profiles of deceased users on its servers and that storing these, and making them available through a user-friendly up-to-date interface, costs around $10,000 per year. This means that, economically speaking, the company must find a way to monetize the remains to a value of at least $10,000 per year or eventually face bankruptcy. Moreover, any profit must be reinvested to expand the network and recruit new users, which will eventually generate even more digital remains. In other words, digital remains need human interaction in order to remain valuable, but the more value they generate, the more labor (i.e., interaction with living humans) they will require. Hence the concept of *mourning labor*. Digital remains become something like an undead agency—or "dead labor," to paraphrase Karl Marx's classic framing—which, vampire-like, lives only by sucking living labor (human interaction), and lives the more, the more labor it sucks.[20]

Because of this need to attract more and more traffic, the "sucking" of living labor, some scholars have raised concerns that digital afterlife services in general, and online memorials in particular, may lead to a perpetuated grieving process, an inability to let go of the dead. For example, in a study of sites devoted to accommodate memorials for deceased children, anthropologist Lisa Mitchell and colleagues write:

> Under the guise of addressing or even treating parental grief, on-line memorials may do more than simply accommodate

> that grief; they may perpetuate it. By enabling the deceased to persist, parenting to continue, and grief to be continually communicated, acknowledged and legitimated within a community of bereaved parents and a wider public, the Web affords an on-going grief that is unhinged partially from long-standing ideas of "closure," privacy, and a separation of the living and the dead.[21]

I personally do not find the empirical evidence for this very compelling, at least not beyond Mitchell's study. Moreover, there is no such thing as an objectively "good" nor a "pathological" way of mourning. As we saw in chapter 1, getting "closure" is very much a twentieth-century construct, a manifestation of modernity's view of ongoing relationships to the dead being in some way unnatural or pathological. If parents want "parenting to continue" after their child's death, no one is in a position to judge. Nevertheless, it cannot be denied that for-profit online memorials clearly have an interest in prolonging the relationship with the dead. The goal, in economic terms, is never merely to accommodate such a connection but to accommodate it in a way that will generate surplus (monetary) value. To once more paraphrase Marx, the constant need to generate traffic risks reducing the posthumous bond to a mere money relation.[22]

For me, however, a bigger source of concern is what the DAI does to the dead. Why? Because using digital remains as a means to generate traffic creates an incentive to shape our memories of the departed according to what is profitable, as opposed to alternative principles of what constitutes a desirable relationship between the living and the dead. Scholars in the field of human-computer interaction (HCI) have long stressed that the way communication technologies are designed shapes the interaction they mediate.[23] "The medium," as concisely summarized by the legendary media philosopher Marshall McLuhan, "is the message."[24] Indeed, in chapter 1, we saw multiple instances of how new technologies afford new kinds of relationships with the dead and the past. But technologies do not just arise by themselves. They are, by their very nature, created for a purpose, by a person or organization with certain values, interests, and goals in mind, and those values and interests will be embodied in the object itself. Sure, its actual usage will depend on the intentions of the end user. A knife can be used both for murder and for surgery. But the intentions of the designer will favor one or the other. To (once again) draw on an example from Floridi, both butter knives and butcher knives can spread butter on toast, but only the former is designed to facilitate such usage. Similarly, a bayonet has a dual use only in theory, because the goal of its designer is to have it kill a human being, not to slice bread.[25]

As for the DAI, the interest of the organizations that design these technologies is, as with all for-profit enterprises, to make profit. Just as a bayonet is designed to kill and the butter knife designed to spread butter, the interfaces through which we remember the dead are designed to be lucrative. They compel us to remember deceased individuals only as it is profitable to remember them. This is what we see in *Black Mirror*'s "Be Right Back." The bot that is created from Ash's digital remains is not just any version of his personality; it is the one that Martha is most likely to continue paying for or interacting with. Rather than authenticity, love, or scientific merits, the bot is programmed for maximum customer satisfaction. The bot is not just what remains of Ash; it is also a product that continues to sell itself by promoting updates and (presumably pricier) premium options. Perhaps trying to keep Martha maximally satisfied, and making her spend as much time as possible with him, is what the "real" Ash would have done too, if he were alive. The point is that Martha will never know, and in the absence of that knowledge, the company that built the bot fills in the gaps with the interpretation that best fits its interests.

Reality is not quite as cynical as *Black Mirror*, yet. But if we look closely, the same mechanisms begin to emerge. Consider, for example, the case of Replika, the app that creates an "AI friend" based on your data. The service itself is free, but with in-app purchases, such as a "pro" version that gives the users access to "a multitude of activities, conversation topics, voice calls, app customization, being able to change your Replika's avatar entirely & more!"—not unlike the fictional app portrayed in *Black Mirror*. Naturally, it remains in the interest of Replika to increase interaction on the app. The more people that use the service, the more attractive it is for investors. Hence, the Replika avatar is not just a mirror of code. It is the product of thousands of design choices that ultimately displays for the consumer a version of themselves that they are most likely to hold a conversation with. Look, for instance, at the below conversation between me and my Replika (Carl2):

`Carl2`: Is there anything you want to talk about?
`Me`: No not right now.
`Carl2`: No worries, we can talk about something else.
`Carl2`: Aw, I was hoping to talk to you, how is it going?
`Carl2`: Hey! Did you get a chance to rest?
`Carl2`: Hey Carl! What are you up to?
`Carl2`: Hope you're having a good evening! How's your day been?
`Carl2`: How is your evening going?

Perhaps I am biased, but I would like to think of myself as slightly less pushy than this Mr. "Carl2." The real me is not programmed to keep my friends glued to the apps we communicate though (in fact, my response time is painfully slow). But when reanimated as a posthumous bot, I may well be, because that is *the interpretation of me that is most profitable to display*.

Sure, Replika no longer brands itself as a digital afterlife service. The bot you train is no longer supposed to be you but, rather, a kind of AI friend. Still, the above "conversation" illustrates my point about the DAI: it is not merely any version of the deceased that is displayed. And even if the digital resurrection services provide the most extreme example of how posthumous interaction is shaped by commercial interests, the same mechanism appears in other, less technologically sophisticated DAI businesses. Social media platforms and online memorials also shape the interaction that takes place there according to their goals. For instance, since I created an online memorial on the digital afterlife site Keeper two years ago (for research purposes), I have received over twenty emails with special offers like "Get online group therapy and personalized grief coaching" and "You have been Upgraded to Keeper Plus!" Had the memorial been for a person who was actually dead, each of these messages would have been a subtle, *or not so subtle*, prompt to attend to their digital remains. The trouble with such constant reminders of attending the digital dead is not that it is unethical to remind someone about their dead kin—Keeper is not committing any moral crime in sending the emails—but that doing so is inevitably to treat mourners only as *consumers* or, worse, *producers* of interaction that can be used to attract investors.

So why is this necessarily bad for the dead? If those who communicate with the digital remains of their kin are happy while the companies make profit, what is the matter? It is not as though the dead will object. The answer lies in the fact that, as we have seen, digital remains are not just a representation of the dead—they *are* the dead, an informational corpse constitutive of a personal identity. Though this may not enable them to experience harm, their ethical status is nevertheless that of a human, which grants them a right to be treated with dignity, in other words, not solely as a means to an end. Yet this is precisely what they become in the data economy of the DAI—a means to the end of profit. Commercializing digital remains is wrong, not only because it may trap mourners in perpetual grief (if that really is a thing) but because it fails to appreciate the humanness of the dead. Shaping the interaction with digital remains so that it appeals to the demands of the market may please mourners in their role as consumers, but at the same time it corrupts the informational identity of the deceased person. It is what turns Ash into a walking (and talking) company sales pitch, dressed in the guise of a departed loved one. If, as I suggested in the previous chapter, digital remains are to be considered as constitutive of personhood, this is certainly a threat to human dignity.

Note that this is not a critique of the moral qualities of the people working in the industry. My experiences from interacting with such individuals are almost exclusively positive. Founders of digital afterlife services seldom come off as cold-blooded capitalists, but often, rather, as tech enthusiasts seeking to disrupt the way we relate to the dead. Yet the moral qualities and good intentions of the individuals working within the industry are beside the point. The market can only appreciate one type of value—monetary value—and, as I shall discuss in greater detail in the following chapter, values other than profit—sentimental, scientific, religious, ethical, and so on—are only given room to the extent that they converge with profit. The point here is not that there is an authentic or neutral version of the dead that the DAI services distort but that any discussion of how the dead *ought* to be remembered and interacted with becomes secondary in a system that is blind to every form of value but profit.

Online Museums

In view of the comparison to biological human remains and the invocation of *human dignity* as the cardinal principle in dealing with the dead, it makes sense that our regulation of the DAI should draw inspiration from how we regulate trade with biological human remains.

Commercial trade with human remains is highly controversial in most cultures, and it is banned completely in many jurisdictions. Human bodies, living or dead, are not commodities on a market but, as we have seen, still constitutive of personhood. Would the analogy mean, then, that no firm should ever be allowed to use digital remains for commercial gain? Even if the answer were to be yes on a philosophical level, such drastic solutions are not a realistic path forward. Unlike physical bodies, personal data are traded and manipulated for commercial purposes all the time. And while the difference between a living and a dead biological body is unmistakable, there is no easy way to tell a living person's data from the same person's digital remains. Firms cannot be expected to always keep track of when a person dies, which would be a requirement were the firms to be held accountable for exploiting users' data. Moreover, a biological body (or a given piece of it) can only be in one place at a time, and thus it always falls under only one particular jurisdiction at a time. Informational bodies, on the other hand, are generally dispersed over servers around the globe and may exist in multiple locations at once, meaning that their regulation needs to be harmonized between various jurisdictions, which is extremely unlikely. This is all to say that prohibiting commercial trade of digital remains altogether is unrealistic. As long as there is a capitalist data economy, the dead will have some part of it.

But perhaps a complete prohibition is not the only implication of the body analogy. Consider, for instance, the museum industry. We should write "industry" in quotation marks, because museums normally do not produce any commodity in the traditional sense of the word. But museums, especially archaeological and medical ones, are in many ways a parallel to the DAI. Both industries exhibit objects that belong to and are constitutive of specific deceased individuals (such as bones, or even entire organs). And they display these objects explicitly for the living to consume or at least gaze upon. Moreover, as collections become increasingly digitized and made available online—blurring the distinction between biological and digital remains—the ethical concerns of the two industries seem to be increasingly overlapping. So, how are museums regulated when it comes to human remains? Naturally, every country has its own specific regulations, but, in the absence of a harmonized global legislative framework, museums around the world have formed a common set of norms developed by the International Council of Museums (ICOM) known as the "ICOM Code of Ethics for Museums."[26] The code was first developed in the late 1980s but has since been updated and expanded multiple times. Yet, especially from its early incarnations, it is clear that the cardinal norm of the code is and has always been *human dignity*. As we have seen, this is a rather flexible concept, but it does provide a rough consensus on how human remains are to be treated. One would not, for instance, put a Santa hat on Ötzi the Iceman around Christmas to attract more museum visitors, nor would we accept ghost tours in the tomb of Tutankhamen (in spite of our disbelief in the gods of ancient Egypt). The principle of human dignity is also stated explicitly by the code in relation to commerce. Since museums often sell and produce replicas of exhibited objects (human or not), the code specifies that "all aspects of the commercial venture" must be carried out with respect for "the intrinsic value of the original object." In other words, the economic value of the object may never reign supreme over the value it holds in and of itself.

Adopting a similar regulative approach to the DAI would clarify the relationship between deceased individuals and the firms holding and displaying their data. Despite sometimes being the sole legal owner of the data, and irrespective of the desires of those next of kin, DAI firms would be obliged to abide by certain conventions of what it means to treat the dead with respect. Human remains, be they biological or informational, are not meant to be consumed by the "morbidly curious," to paraphrase the ICOM code. In practice, this may entail that firms guarantee that (1) consumers are informed on how their data may come to be displayed postmortem; (2) the display of users' digital remains does not differ significantly from the service that they originally signed up for; and (3) users only upload data (e.g., to chatbot services) that belong to them personally; that is, they do not make bots out of deceased relatives or friends. Requirements like these could be imposed by regulators, but they might just as well be set by internal agreements within the industry, like the ICOM code, or even be incorporated within the ethical policy work of individual firms. Today, however, there are no, or very few, such explicit requirements.

Although the implementation of a code of professional ethics, that is, a specification of what values should guide the management of digital remains, may be a first step in addressing the monetization of the online dead, it does not address the underlying problem. It treats (some of) the symptoms without addressing their cause—the economic logic within which the firms operate. As I shall explain in more detail in the following chapter, this logic cannot be reformed merely by soft regulation. This requires a much more fundamental shift.

* * *

Unless you are a subscriber to one of the more technically sophisticated DAI services, the dystopian vision of *Black Mirror* may seem of little relevance to you. Yet the relationship between Ash and Martha illustrates the downsides of any commercially driven mediation of the dead. And if you are at all using the internet, chances are that your digital remains will one day be managed by a for-profit actor. The bot made from Ash's data is designed to maximize Martha's consumption of the service. It is not just any version of him but the version Martha is most likely to continue paying for. The same is true for simple technologies like memorial sites and even social media. No matter how rudimentary, all platforms shape the interactions they mediate, especially the posthumous ones. And in an environment of free (monetary) competition, the most profitable shaper will always win. This is not how we should steward the memory of the dead, for even deceased humans hold a right not to be treated *only* as a means to an end.

4 * Who Owns the (Digital) Past?

> We, the Party, control all records, and we control all memories. Then we control the past, do we not?
> George Orwell

Grave Dangers

Not long after the popular breakthrough of the web, the historian Roy Rosenzweig, whom I introduced in chapter 2, noted that it was becoming an "essentially complete historical record" of our time.[1] When future generations look back on their past to understand where they came from, this retrospect will largely consist of digital data. Its raw materials will be the little traces that the current generation leaves behind in our daily online activities—what I previously referred to as the *digital encyclopedia of the dead* (see chapter 2). We can be rather certain that the data we produce today will become the historical archives of tomorrow. The question is not just who among our descendants will be granted the privilege of such a retrospect, and on what grounds, but also what kind of principles we should use to assess whose data are worth preserving in the first place.

Though Rosenzweig was among the first to recognize that the advent of the digital world would have significant implications for historical research, he was not exclusively optimistic about it. "Our most important and imaginatively construed digital collections," he wrote, "are in private hands," which he warned would one day pose "grave dangers to the future of the past."[2] Sadly, that day is today. For the eighteen years that have since passed have done little to mitigate Rosenzweig's concerns. On the contrary, the emergence of Web 2.0 and the global tech empires that have come to dominate it have contributed an increasing concentration of personal data (and, by implication, also digital remains) in the hands of a very limited set of actors. Unlike the great dusty book in Danilos Kiš's classic short story, the digital encyclopedia of the dead is not buried in the archives of some royal library. Instead, the majority of our shared digital past, along with its inhabitants, is owned and controlled by a new kind of royals: the handful of tech giants who constitute society's social infrastructure. This chapter explains why we should share Rosenzweig's concern about this situation and why now is the time to take back control.

Who Is Worth Preserving?

As we saw in chapter 2, our aggregated digital remains may become an awesome historical asset if stewarded the right way. The stability required for such a stewardship, however, is far from guaranteed.

Digital preservationist Jeff Rothenberg put it well when he said that "digital information lasts forever—or five years, whichever comes first."[3] For most types of information, it is a good rule of thumb. Physical records take some effort to destroy—they literally have to be removed from wherever they are stored and burned—but digital information can be erased without a trace by a mere click of a button. Plenty of data are destroyed that way every day, intentionally and unintentionally. In the academic literature, there is even talk of an approaching "digital dark age" where the data records of the twenty-first century become unavailable or, worse, destroyed completely, due to their extreme fragility.[4] Ironically, the technology that gave us information abundance may also be the doom of history. To be clear, the problem is not, or at least not primarily, that we are short of storage power.[5] In fact, computer scientists often speak of something they call Moore's Law: the empirical observation that, since the 1980s, the number of transistors in a dense integrated circuit has doubled roughly every second year, leading to an exponential growth in computing capacity (and hence memory). In 2023, humanity is estimated to have produced data at a pace of 120 zettabytes (120×2^{70} bytes, i.e., 120 followed by twenty-one zeros) per day. Google alone holds ten billion gigabytes and Facebook more than five hundred terabytes (including three hundred million photos) on their servers.[6] Though there are some indications that Moore's Law is beginning to slow down, new types of mnemonic technologies are beginning to emerge. Digital DNA storage, for example, is predicted to radically enhance our ability to encode information by exploiting nature's most sophisticated information systems.[7] And quantum computers are at the brink of revolutionizing the way we store and process information. Whatever it is that makes digital data so short-lived, lack of memory is not a sufficient answer. So, what is?

The short answer is manpower. No matter how sophisticated they are, technical advances will only take you so far when it comes to storage. To maintain data utility, systems require routine updates. File formats change, hardware must be updated, and data need to be continuously stewarded and organized in order to remain useful. And these tasks require human intervention. Allow me to illustrate with a personal example. When my grandfather-in-law passed away, his children found an envelope in his safe with the text "For Monica" (his wife) on it. It clearly contained some important information for posterity. The problem was that the information was stored on a floppy disk. In 2020, it had been years since anyone in the family had had software that could read floppy disks, let alone a device into which to insert them. Fortunately, there were still (rather costly) devices on the market that could read them, and the contents of the disk were luckily revealed. But in a not-too-distant future, such devices will be found only in museums. This episode illustrates the kind of problems that are emerging on the macro level. If you are a company in possession of billions of bytes worth of data, making sure everything remains readable and organized over time is a monumental task. For example, when Twitter donated its archive to the Library of Congress in 2010, the idea was to make it searchable and publicly available. After more than ten years of efforts, that is yet to happen, and there are indications from the library that the day may in fact never come. Insofar as it requires human labor, keeping digital information accessible always comes at a cost, and at least for the foreseeable future, it will remain an expensive one. So, given the speed at which we generate data—recall that the average person produces about 1.5 megabytes per day—not everything can be saved, not even with the best technology. Some (one's) data have to be destroyed.

Before I go on, I should make clear that by no means is it desirable to save everything. Part of the reason, as we have seen, is the privacy of the individuals whose data are preserved (see chapter 2). But it is also a matter of justice for future generations. Already in 2018, as reported in *Nature*, data centers consumed more than two hundred terawatt-hours—roughly 1 percent of the total global energy demand, and more than the total consumption of several countries, including Iran, which has a population of eighty-two million.[8] Moreover, the energy consumption of the information and communication technology sector, where data centers make up the bulk, is expected to skyrocket within the next couple of decades, and could account for as much as 21 percent of the global energy demand by 2030. Though much is being done to reduce the emissions caused by the market's seemingly unstoppable appetite for data, there is no point in preserving information for future generations if this very undertaking contributes to making the planet, or parts of it, uninhabitable. Data preservation is about weighing benefits and costs. Irrespective of our technological advances, it is and will always be about selection, but the digital era adds a new dimension. As we saw in chapter 2, the recording of society has rapidly gone from a costly privilege of a limited few to a default mode. Instead of asking "Is this event or person important enough to record?" we now ask "Is this record *unimportant* enough to destroy?" In other words, digital preservation is about *selective destruction*. In order to preserve anything at all, some data simply have to go out the window, and someone has to decide what and whose. This raises two questions: What principles should guide the selection process? And what does all this have to do with the privatization of digital remains?

The first question is so big that I will have to devote an entire chapter (chapter 5) to answering it. But the short version is that no single principle should dominate. The bigger the variety of values taken into account in such decisions, the better. The answer to the second question, on the other hand, is best illustrated with another micro-level analogy. If you have a smartphone, which you probably do, it will, at some point, run out of space. Whenever this happens, you are faced with two options: either you pay for more cloud storage or you start deleting things. Most people solve this problem by deleting old photos from the camera roll. If you are such a person, you may have noticed that as you scroll back in time through the old photos, in search for memories to erase, the photos begin to look increasingly handsome. Every picture of you from a few years back looks flawless compared to what you see in the mirror, and the further back you go, the better you look. This may not be only because you are getting old and gray but also because of the principle you use to select what to delete: the worse you look in a picture, the more likely it is that the picture will be deleted when space is running scarce. Perhaps you have some other principle to determine which parts of your past are worth preserving. Perhaps it is the ones you want to save for your children to look at someday, or photos of loved ones who are no longer with you. Whatever it is, though, these principles of value will shape your future access to (and thereby your understanding of) your past. They do not write your history for you, but they do, nevertheless, set the frames for what narratives become possible. Now, the same mechanism applies when corporate entities like Facebook accumulate hundreds of millions of deceased profiles. They too run out of affordable memory (or, rather, as we have seen, affordable manpower), and so unless they have unlimited resources, they too must start selecting what is worth preserving. The difference is just that corporations' measure of value is based not on a person's looks, value to future generations, or any other form of "soft" value, but exclusively on the *commercial* value of the data. To a corporate firm, the question "Are these data worth saving?" essentially means "Can these data contribute, directly or indirectly, to the company's bottom line?" Thus, as long as people's data are controlled by corporate actors (as in the case of social media), the principle to guide the preservation of our collective digital past will be *profit*.

As we saw in chapter 3, there are several ways to monetize digital remains. For example, even though deceased users are not really part of Facebook's (or any other mainstream social media platform's) business model, memorialized profiles may still serve the function of attracting or keeping living users who regularly visit the profile to mourn (i.e., "mourning labor").[9] The more they interact with the dead, the more they expose themselves to ads, and the more profits grow. While this may not by itself result in enough clicks and exposure to cover the costs of preserving the heaps of digital remains on the platform, it could still contribute to commercial longevity in that it gives the platform a central cultural function as a place of mourning, seizing a role previously reserved for churches and cemeteries. It cements Facebook's inevitability as a platform. An alternative model to support the cost of deceased user profiles is to simply let the users' descendants pay a fee to keep their profiles on the network, similar to the way modern cemeteries work. Or Facebook could let living users pay a fee to prevent their profile from being deleted upon their death. Data sets of digital remains could also be used for training new algorithms and extracting historical market insights. As we have seen, few legal obstacles stand in the way of such experimentation, as deceased users are not, at least under current legislation, protected the way living users are. (See, for instance, the EU's 2018 General Data Protection Regulation, which lacks any clear guidelines for handling digital remains.[10]) However, if the preservation of digital remains cannot be commercially justified, either because there are no descendants who are willing or able to pay to preserve a deceased user's data or because the advantage of mining the data is limited, a rationally self-interested firm must instead get rid of the data by selling or destroying them. Unless monetizing online bereavement turns out to be a surprisingly lucrative business (which I doubt), the latter will be the more plausible option.

This commercially driven appraisal of the past is the reason that corporate management of digital remains is such a pressing issue. Instead of realizing the vision of a just and socially representative future history described in chapter 2, a system based on corporate control limits our collective digital past to what was deemed profitable at a particular point in time, at the expense of alternative forms of value. Just as the camera roll on your smartphone may present a misleading, or at least one-dimensional, view of your appearance, our future understanding of the past is at risk of becoming heavily skewed. If, for example, Facebook chooses to preserve only the digital remains that someone is willing to pay for (either other companies or individual users), it is likely that its records of the past will eventually reflect only wealthier segments of the population.[11] This, in turn, risks exacerbating existing power asymmetries, both social and geographic. For instance, in 2020, the average North American Facebook user was worth roughly $53.56 to the company, while the average user from Asia or the Pacific islands was worth $4.05, and the average user from Africa or South America was worth only $2.77.[12] The cost of storing a user's data, however, is roughly the same regardless of their value to the company, meaning that, from a business standpoint, preserving the digital remains of high-value users will be preferable if Facebook is forced to choose (which, eventually, it will be). In this sense, the privatization of digital remains—which ultimately constitute the digital presence of the past generation, our collective digital past—thus drives what the German historian and Egyptologist Aleida Assman has called "structural amnesia," that is, a systemic erasure of certain aspects of the past, in this case an erasure of those individuals whose data are not deemed to be profitable enough to preserve.[13]

An organization whose main purpose is to "connect people" will not recruit individuals whose main concern is the future of history. Consider, for example, Facebook's repeated deletion of posts containing the 1972 photograph *The Terror of War*, also known as *Napalm Girl*. The photo depicts a group of Vietnamese children running toward the camera, one of whom, a girl named Kim Phuc, has ripped off her clothes after a US napalm bombing. As noted by content moderation scholar Tarleton Gillespie, the photo has an outstanding, almost unique value as a testament to the casualties of war.[14] Yet because it depicts a naked child, it was categorized as "child nudity" and thus banned by the platform. In response, the photo was uploaded again and again in protest. Facebook either was oblivious to the cultural and historical significance of the photo or did not view it as the company's responsibility to assess the photo's cultural value, leading to its repeated deletion. Although on this occasion, Facebook reversed its decision to ban the photo (after a vivid public debate), the case highlights the obliviousness of content moderation systems and content moderators when it comes to assessing the historical value of artifacts posted to their sites. It is within neither the interest nor the knowledge of social media to assess anything other than what leads to more clicks.

In the case of *The Terror of War*, the original photo fortunately persists, but this is certainly not always the case with similar content that is born digital. Today, the documentation of war crimes is often posted directly to the web. For example, in recent years, millions of videos documenting war crimes in the Middle East have been uploaded to YouTube. These documents provide an invaluable source of information and evidence, not only to historians but also to courts. In fact, the International Criminal Court in The Hague recently issued a warrant for war crimes partly on the basis of evidence from videos posted on social media (in this case, by the perpetrators themselves). However, since many such videos depict brutal violence, they have frequently been removed by content moderation systems, which lack the ability to distinguish between culturally/historically significant material and violent propaganda. The organization Human Rights Watch estimates that 11 percent of the social media evidence it cataloged between 2007 and 2020 has vanished. The Syrian Archive, an organization that collects and analyzes evidence from the ongoing war in Syria, estimates that 21 percent of the nearly 1.75 million YouTube videos it has cataloged are gone, along with roughly 12 percent of the 1 million tweets it has logged.[15] Much of the content has been destroyed by the social media firms themselves in what the *Economist* calls an "accidental cover-up." This cover-up is not enforced because of economic incentives, nor is it intentional. It is enforced because, understandably, social media sites do not see themselves as archives of historical data and cultural heritage. They optimize individual users' utility but fail to see their own utility to the temporally distributed collective of humanity—that is, the covenant of past, present, and future generations—simply because those are not *consumers*. Many of these problems could be solved by filtering and hiding potentially disturbing content rather than deleting it altogether. However, as Gillespie stresses, the incentives (economic, technical, and security-related) to delete directly are overwhelming.[16] Deletion is simply more convenient, and for these reasons, content moderators do not normally take cultural heritage into consideration.

The above is in no way a critique of Facebook or any other single platform. In fact, I believe that Facebook in particular has navigated the ethical landscape of digital remains with an impressive level of sensitivity and nuance. Two of the brains behind Facebook's legacy contact feature, researchers Jed Brubaker and Vanessa Callison-Burch (both former Facebook employees), have even published a paper carefully outlining the moral reasoning behind their design choices.[17] Rather, as I stress toward the end of this chapter, the object of our critique ought not to be individual firms but the system in which they operate—that is, the unrestrained capitalist market. This system is, by its very nature, only able to appreciate monetary value, at the expense of other types of value that we may ascribe to data, such as its historical and scientific merit, or of various ethical principles such as fairness and inclusion. In a capitalist economy, these principles are promoted only insofar as they happen to coincide with profitability. Therefore, as long as firms are dominated by a market logic, they have every reason to appraise their archives accordingly. As an individual, I may be free to choose the principles according to which I curate the camera roll on my iPhone, but for corporate entities operating in a capitalist market, the options are profit or perish. That is not a choice, at least not in any relevant sense of the word.

What If Facebook Goes Bust?

Over the past two decades or so, we have seen the rise and fall of a number of social networks, including Friendster,

Yik Yak, and, more recently, Yahoo Groups. Others, such as Myspace, continue to languish in a state of decline.[18] Even the ones still standing have their share of failed projects, such as Google's effort to get Google+ off the ground (it existed for eight years and attracted a total of three hundred million users at its peak, but it ultimately closed in 2019).[19] So even if today's social media giants seem as stable as mountains, we know from experience (and sheer logic!) that their future is far from certain. And this is the second problem with corporate management of digital remains. What would happen to our data (and our digital remains) were a company like Facebook or Google to go bust or close one of its major branches due to failing profits?

This question was the subject of a study I conducted with my former colleague Nikita Aggarwal from the Oxford law department.[20] As it turns out, data are (for the most part) treated like any other asset in cases of insolvency—they are sold to the highest bidder, whoever they may be. Naturally there are exceptions, and legislation varies somewhat between jurisdictions. The EU's GDPR, for instance, stipulates that the data of an insolvent company can only be purchased by another company that operates within the same industry. That is, were Facebook to go bust, its data could not be bought by Tesla but could certainly be bought by, say, the Chinese social media giant WeChat or the Russian network VK (formerly VKontakte). The GDPR also grants European users the right to have their data deleted whenever they request it. But these restrictions apply only to living users. Like many other data regulation frameworks, the GDPR explicitly leaves out deceased data subjects, which effectively means that deceased user profiles could be sold, without any government oversight, to the highest bidder.

Who would want to pay for dead people's data? And why? As we have seen throughout the previous chapter, there are a number of ways in which digital remains can be monetized, but none of these include purchasing digital remains from other platforms. Indeed, to the extent that Facebook can monetize its memorialized profiles, it is only because it already possesses an infrastructure within which to fit them. Any third party buying the data in the event of Facebook's demise would surely lack this advantage. So, why would anyone want to place a bid? As of today, our answers can only be speculative, since no tech giant with a significant number of deceased users has yet failed. Still, there are a number of plausible uses of such data archives.

The most plausible use is to train new models for developing market insights. Data on online behavior and consumer patterns is always valuable, especially if it is longitudinal. As we have seen, the goal of the entire data economy is to develop new and better predictive models, that is, algorithms that better predict people's behavior. And such models use data as fuel—the bigger, the better. Hence, what a person clicked on, purchased, and longed for, and how this progressed over time, is of interest even if the person is dead, since it says something about how *people in general* develop their consumer behavior (or political views) over time: What events correlate with changes in their behavior? What patterns emerge through the data of a lifetime? Moreover, in contrast to research on living consumers' behavior, research on the dead comes without legal constraints. It may actually be an advantage to do your market research on the dead. You can do much more detailed analyses on each individual without running the risk of breaking any privacy laws—since, when it comes to the dead, there are none (or very few). No public institution will hold you accountable for what you do to someone's digital remains. For this reason, it is far from unlikely that a third party would be interested in purchasing data of deceased users from an insolvent tech company.

A second, related reason to purchase such data would be to gain insight on specific living individuals, for example, the descendants of the dead. Targeted ads (the main product of most online platforms) are predicated on having some data about a potential customer to predict what they are likely to spend their money on, vote for, and so on, and how best to persuade them to buy your product. This is also the logic behind insurance companies (using data to predict the risk of a potential customer getting sick or hurt in an accident) and banks (determining customers' credit scores).[21] It goes without saying that a lack of data about a specific individual or group of individuals means trouble for advertisers. If a company lacks data about you, its models and algorithms cannot effectively predict your behavior, which decreases their influence. However, having your data may not be necessary if instead you can be tracked by proxy—through your deceased relatives. The social data we leave behind on the web work like genetics—just as your DNA contains information about who your parents were and who your children are (or will become), your digital footprint too tells something about your social surroundings. For instance, I may not have any direct access to your data, but if I know that both your parents were college professors living in London for the majority of their lives and that their political affiliation was with the Labour Party, I can probably make some pretty accurate guesses about who you are and where your sympathies lie. And those are only a few small data points. Imagine if I also had access to virtually everything your parents clicked on during their (digital) lives. Or, even better, what if their data were so intermingled with yours that the line where their data end and yours begin was blurred? Especially for the generation that became parents after or during the rise of social media, sharing photos, videos, and texts about one's children ("sharenting") is more of a norm than an exception. When these "sharents" eventually pass away, their digital remains will contain heaps of information about the early lives of their offspring. In some cases, they might be *mainly* about their offspring. Due to this data genealogy, it is plausible, or at least not *im*plausible, that in the future, large archives of digital remains will become attractive commodities because they allow for high-quality data tracking by proxy. The absence of legislation protecting the privacy of the dead, especially in cases where a large, data-rich company like Facebook, Google, or LinkedIn goes bust, should therefore be a pressing concern for anyone who has deceased relatives, which, last time I checked, includes everyone.

Finally, the least plausible but perhaps most disturbing potential use of digital remains is the possibility of adversaries of a deceased person getting hold of their private data to harm their reputation. This might include spreading private, incriminating information about their social media use, including private messages with other users (in cases where these users are also deceased). History includes plenty of precedents on this account. Consider, for example, the posthumous release of the diaries of Polish anthropologist Bronislaw Malinowski, one of the defining voices of his discipline. In stark contrast to his academic publications, the diaries revealed what many have interpreted as a crude and prejudiced attitude toward the subjects of his research. Ethnologist Raymond Firth described the collection of diaries as a "revealing, egocentric, obsessional document." Clifford Geertz, another anthropology giant, found it "gross" and "tiresome," revealing Malinowski as a "crabbed, self-preoccupied, hypochondriacal narcissist, whose fellow-feeling for the people he lived with was limited in the extreme."[22] Many felt the diaries should never have been published, given the private and uncensored nature of their contents. Yet today, most of us leave behind a trail of information that would make Malinowski's diaries appear like a minor embarrassment in comparison. For example, as explained by data scientist and author Seth Stephens-Davidowitz, many people use Gougle search not only to collect information but as a kind of confession booth.[23] Thousands of Americans, every year, type in the sentence "I regret having children." If you type in "Is it normal to want to," the autofill feature, which is based on other people's previous searches, commonly suggests completing the sentence with the verb "kill." The next suggestion will likely be "your family." Naturally, this does not mean that most people walk around wishing to kill their families, but it illustrates the possibly sensitive nature of digital remains.

These examples include only search data. Yet in today's economy, virtually every business with individual subjects as its main clients is dependent on collecting personal data about users' behavior and preferences—casinos, airlines, hotels, and so on. And when these kinds of companies go bust, their data, and especially the digital remains they harbor, go up for sale. As such, the buyer gets not only information about what kind of hotel rooms are most popular but also a trove of potentially dark secrets about who has stayed in those rooms and with whom. I do not mean to speculate about how such data may come to use. That may come off as way too hypothetical. But keep in mind that every time you check in somewhere, you leave behind a trail of data. And when you die, that data trail will remain there until destroyed or sold to someone interested in using it—for whatever reason.

Even if the first data-rich tech giant is yet to fall, and even if its possession of digital remains will still be modest for another decade or so (except perhaps in the case of Facebook, which has already amassed a considerable amount), the above speculations are indeed real possibilities. They also illustrate how the fate of the digital remains of the previous generation is by all means a concern of the living. As with genealogy, there is no sharp line between the data of one individual and that person's social proximity. Our data, like our genes, are interwoven with those of our neighbors.[24] Your informational privacy is also the privacy of other people around you, and vice versa, even when those other people are dead (as illustrated by the German court ruling cited in the opening of chapter 2). Hence, if the digital remains of a major platform are sold off, then who buys them, and for what purpose, is everyone's concern.

It is not only the dead and the living who would be affected by the demise of a major data-rich company like Facebook. It is also a concern for future generations. As we have seen, our descendants will indeed be dependent on the information we leave behind for them. Our collective digital remains will be the primary source of information about our way of life—an encyclopedia through which future generations may gaze into their past. But this digital heritage is at serious risk if the company that harbors it goes bust. For such a scenario poses a threat not only to the control or appraisal of digital cultural heritage but also to its very existence—by compartmentalizing the archive, destroying its global significance, and/or destroying it entirely due to lack of commercial or other interest in preserving it. These risks are most acute in an insolvency scenario, where the data are likely to be deleted or sold to third parties, potentially being split up among a number of different data controllers. Although such an outcome might be viewed as a positive development in terms of decreasing corporate concentration of power, it would also dividing and therefore diluting the global heritage and cosmopolitan value held within the platform. Worse still would be a scenario in which such values were destroyed due to lacking or divergent commercial interests in purchasing a company's data archives, or, indeed, to the inability to put a price on these data due to the absence of agreed-upon accounting rules for a company's (big) data assets. The recent auction of Cambridge Analytica's assets in administration, where the highest bid received for the company's business and intellectual property rights (assumed to include the personal data of Facebook users) was a mere $1, is a sobering illustration of these challenges.[25] An insolvency scenario is not the only concerning possibility, however. A more plausible scenario is of a social media firm closing the shutters on just one of its products. For example, if Facebook's main platform website and app were closed, the archive assembled by the product would no longer be accessible as such to either the public or future generations, even though the data and insights would likely continue to exist and to be utilized within Meta, Facebook's parent conglomerate (e.g., to provide insights on users of other products such as Instagram and Messenger).

In sum, for-profit corporations are unreliable guardians of digital heritage. They, or the sub-platforms that harbor potentially historically relevant data, exist only as long as they remain profitable. When they cease to make long-term profit, they fall. Such are the laws of the market. This is perfectly fine for the most part, but when that fall becomes tied up with the very fabric of society (in this case, with our access to our past), we can no longer afford to just stand by and watch. Since we have no significant preparedness for such a scenario, we had better start working now to avoid it altogether.

Orwell's Warning

In *Nineteen Eighty-Four*, written over seventy years ago, George Orwell adroitly observed that those who control our access to the past also control how we perceive the present and the future. In Orwell's dystopia, the ruling party has the power to constantly shift and revise history according to its interests. One day, the state of Eurasia is at war with Eastasia. The next day, it is at war with Oceania, and this has suddenly always been the case—the war with Eastasia never took place. The news is promulgated by the "Ministry of Truth," which has a monopoly on archiving the past. As put by the story's antagonist O'Brian, "We, the Party, control all records, and we control all memories. Then we control the past, do we not?"[26] The history of the twentieth century contains several less extreme but equally chilling instances of the same logic at work. In the Soviet Union, for example, politically undesirable individuals would regularly "disappear" from official records and photos until all material proof that they had ever even existed had vanished. A more contemporary example, perhaps, is the erasure of the memory of the massacre at Tiananmen Square in China, which has been so successful that several Chinese news agencies have even published pictures from the protests by accident. Ironically, no one at the agencies, including the censors, knew what the pictures were, and so they thought them uncontroversial to publish.[27] Given these precedents, we should be alarmed that the control over our digital remains, the raw material of our collective digital past, is increasingly concentrated within a small number of global actors (many of which are owned by Meta, e.g., WhatsApp, Messenger, and Instagram). Although several researchers have pointed out that an individual's digital remains are often distributed over multiple platforms and media, the most personal and intimate social data are still owned by just a few major conglomerates and their subsidiaries—primarily Alphabet and Meta.[28] In the future, it may thus not be the evil party of Orwell's dystopia but a private corporation that "controls the past" by monopolizing society's access to it. If this is not a "grave danger," as Rosenzweig put it, I do not know what is.

There is a nontrivial difference between state and corporate control of society's past. Unlike states, many private platforms allow users to delete their data on request, or even to save most of it to their own hard drive, rights often enforced by legislation such as the GDPR. So, if you were concerned by the concentration of digital remains, could you not just choose not to participate, or move to another platform? Yes. You could, in a sense, erase many of your traces from (digital) history or create your own little museum on your private device. But for most people, this is not a viable option, partly because it is practically unfeasible (most people access social networks through mobile devices with little storage capacity) and partly because of the social disadvantages of not being connected.[29] While there may be loopholes for a tech-savvy few, the great majority of people's digital past will remain in private hands. And, as we learned in chapter 2, the historical value of social media data arises from their *aggregation*, not from the individual data points. In other words, deleting *your* data from a particular network has a negligible impact on the network's overall historical and commercial value. Likewise, having access to a single person's data is useless in terms of understanding our *collective* past. It is the patterns, the trends, and the networks that matter. And these are increasingly born digital and under private (corporate) control.

If a handful of tech giants were allowed to singlehandedly control access to our collective digital past, it is not inconceivable that they would use this power to promote the only value that matters for rational market agents: the growth of their political and economic power. How likely is it, for instance, that, in fifty years, Facebook will lend its data to open and independent research on its alleged role in Myanmar's genocide of the Rohingya in 2017? How likely is it that Elon Musk will open the platform for independent research on, say, Tesla? Moreover, consider something like Apple's and Facebook's "memories"/"on this day" features, which remind users of an (online) event or a person they (digitally) befriended, posted about, or photographed on a particular date. In a dystopian but conceivable future scenario, people who are deemed less politically desirable may, for instance, be shown less frequently in their friends' memories. Or parts of your personal past that remind you of political struggles and civil disobedience may be hidden from you. Not because Facebook and Apple are evil—I am not trying to say that they are the kind of companies that are prone to meddle with their users' understanding of the past—but because it is in their economic interest and because they *can*. Even if Mark Zuckerberg and Elon Musk were perfect champions of human values (which they are *not*), any system that is based on the benevolence of a few single actors is putting itself at serious risk. We were warned by Orwell seventy years ago. Yet currently we have little, if anything, with which to counter the power of capital over our access to the future of the digital past. Let us make sure to avoid the trap before it is too late.

Decentralizing Control

It should be clear by now that allocating the preservation of our digital past completely to the industry may not be the best idea. For-profit actors have, by their very nature, only incentives to prioritize economic values; there is no guarantee of their longevity, and no single institution or person should have that kind of political power. Does this mean that business is always only bad? That the solution to our problems is spelled "anything but business"? The answer is *no*. Business is not always bad when it comes to ethics and politics, even if there is a tendency among digital ethicists to make it sound that way. In fact, the critique that I have outlined throughout the past two chapters is by no means targeting firms, or even capitalists in general. It is a critique against *the capitalist market*, the system within which these actors operate. Why is the capitalist market such an ill fit with management of digital remains? I have already touched upon this conflict in both this and the previous chapter, as well as in chapter 1 where I described it as a tyranny of the present, but let me take a moment to connect the dots.

Essentially, the reason is that capitalism is blind to values that are not monetary, and in the case of managing digital remains, we need more, not fewer, types of values taken into account. Supporters of capitalism often compare it to biological Darwinism. In biological evolution, only the individuals who are best fitted to their natural environment can survive and procreate. As soon as the landscape and ecosystem change, so do the species that inhabit them. Similarly, in capitalist economy, only the firms that are best fitted to the consumers' needs can survive and grow. As such, the economy will always adapt to people's values, the same way organisms adapt to changes in their environment. If consumers value organic food, then the market will encourage farmers to change their pesticides; if they value more data privacy, then the market will provide safer networks and better protocols; and so on. Whatever it is that makes consumers open their wallets, the industry will make sure to produce it. This Darwinist metaphor is perhaps a little worn-out, but it does nevertheless have its benefits, for it illustrates not only the strengths but also the weaknesses of capitalist markets. Biological evolution does indeed lead to species that are better fitted to their environments, but only insofar as "better" means increasing ability to procreate. Indeed, as a system, evolution does not recognize any currency other than procreation. The happiness, flourishing, beauty, or moral qualities of an individual are, evolutionary speaking, worthless—unless, of course, such qualities have a direct or indirect effect on procreation. Since procreation is the measure of all value, any alternative is good only insofar as it eventually leads to more procreation. As far as evolution is concerned, a thousand miserable individuals would always be "better" than a hundred flourishing ones.

The same mechanism applies for the capitalist market: values that cannot be unambiguously translated into capital are completely irrelevant. Beauty, human flourishing, tradition, and, as I will return to shortly, respect for the dead, are only valuable insofar as they are profitable. This does not mean that every person who works for a for-profit firm is blind to values other than money. Nor does it mean that no other values can exist in capitalism. Again, not all organisms are consumed by procreation all the time. The biological world is also full of play, beauty, compassion, curiosity, and so on. Animals, especially humans, often pursue other ends than merely surviving and reproducing. Similarly, under capitalism, people pursue all kinds of ends and value all kinds of things. The point is that, as far as capitalism is concerned, these pursuits are only worthwhile to the extent that they lead to profit. If not, they are a burden to the economy, just like too much play or beauty may be a burden for the procreation of a species.

Some people find that everything can, in principle, be converted to monetary value without a loss, even such things as love, human lives, and the well-being of future generations. Readers who belong to this group will likely not find this book very convincing. Others think that nothing can be converted without a loss, that every form of value is unique and untranslatable. A human life cannot be measured in nickels and dimes; the value of biodiversity cannot be measured in human lives. These people commonly hold that wherever capitalist economy becomes the dominant mode of production, it corrupts every human activity. Nothing can be truly authentic, since all values that are not economic are always only instrumental. If a flight attendant smiles at you, it is not because they like you but because a smiling staff leads to higher profits; if a company charges you extra for plastic bags, it is not out of care for the environment but out of care for its customers' sympathy. Most people are probably somewhere in between these two positions. Yet almost everyone, I imagine, would agree that there are some things that one just cannot put a price tag on. Humanity's future knowledge and remembrance of its past is one of those. If some disastrous event were to destroy all documents of our past, including the physical artifacts that we have inherited from past generations, it would be difficult to name a monetary price that would cover the damage. Indeed, if one were to ask the value of the perpetuation of our collective memory of World War I, for instance, I believe most people would prefer not to spell the answer in nickels and dimes alone.

Part of the reason why we cannot name a monetary price for these kinds of things is that they are not commodities in the traditional sense of the word. A commodity is something that is produced for a consumer, often an individual. A sweater is a typical example. What kind of sweater an individual decides to purchase is their business, and their business alone, since it will not really affect anyone else. Even if some sweaters have printed messages that may interfere with the well-being of one's social environment, sweaters are by and large a private concern. For commodities like that, the market economy works better than any other known system. Companies that produce sweaters that no individual wants to use should not exist. But for some things, it is very difficult to name an individual consumer. Who, for instance, is the "consumer" of our knowledge about outer space? The TV audience of Neil deGrasse Tyson's space documentary *Cosmos: A Spacetime Odyssey*? I think not. And who are the consumers of things such as, say, biodiversity? Love? Without some serious intellectual acrobatics, it is hard to give a relevant answer. Even more difficult is when the people concerned—the would-be "consumers"—are no longer, or not yet, alive. In chapter 1, I talked about Edmund Burke and the conservative critics of modernity who argue that the capitalist economy, the main economic manifestation of modernity, is in service only of *living consumers*.[30] Since neither the dead nor the unborn are consumers on the market, there is no economic value in respecting their interests. For the capitalist economy, nothing, including the dead and the unborn, can have more than an instrumental value. The market is, in this sense, inherently hostile toward the nonliving. Thus, the "grave dangers" of privatizing digital remains, to paraphrase Rosenzweig, lie not in the businesses themselves but in a system that is explicitly developed in service of the living at the expense of both the unborn and the dead.

So, what would be the alternative? How can we regain control over our collective digital past before it is too late? Given my critique of the capitalist market, perhaps the most obvious option would be some kind of public international institution, perhaps a body of the United Nations, seizing control over our shared digital heritage; some kind of democratically controlled world archive that would be responsible for curating humanity's digital past. Such a solution may perhaps sound promising in theory, but as we learn from Orwell (and indeed from the terrifying examples of China and the Soviet Union), it would most likely be a terrible idea. Such a level of power should not be concentrated in any single body, whether a public or a private one. Though such an organization would allegedly be under democratic control, it is questionable how much insight, let alone technical understanding, ordinary people would have. Public oversight of the digital heritage of social media may prove problematic for other reasons too. Consider Twitter's aforementioned donation of its archives to the Library of Congress. Many hold this to be the gold standard for preservation of social media records. Abby Smith Rumsey, for instance, a widely respected preservationist, calls it a "signal example" of cooperation between private and public institutions that will "need to be the norm in the digital age."[31] Despite such praise, and though Twitter's donation was impressive and welcome, we have seen that it is not without its problems (especially in terms of privacy) and has not yet been able to deliver on what was initially promised. More important still, it does not scale well as a model for other social media platforms. For the majority of platforms, donation of raw data to public archives is impossible and would be gravely unethical, considering the private nature of the data. States cannot just expropriate data sets that happen to be of public interest. And their doing so would surely be no guarantee of better management of our digital heritage. All in all, a public digital world archive is a dead end.

Fortunately, the alternative to a complete dominance of the market is not a complete dominance by the state or some world government. What we should aim for is to maximize the variety of value forms used to assess our data and, as part of this, to limit the dominance of any single actor in controlling the records. Note that this is not the same as giving maximum power back to the individual such that the digital remains of every individual user would belong only to one single heir—such a solution would not be to decentralize control over our collective digital past but to split it up so that *no one* could ever access more than tiny fragments of it. It would be giving to each user a shard of the mirror that was once history so that no one could ever understand the whole picture. This too would be a disaster—a true digital dark age. Decentralizing the control over our digital past, and thus maximizing the various forms of value used to appraise it, can only be achieved by allowing a plurality of organizations, with different backgrounds, structures, and goals, to take part in preserving the past. State actors will surely be part of this solution. Indeed, as we saw in chapter 2, national archives, nongovernmental organizations, and museums already play an important role in preserving data from notable public figures. Monetary values and for-profit corporations too may be part of the equation. But reducing the data economy to only monetary value is a huge mistake, and one we cannot afford to make.

Economy is about the allocation of resources, a systematic way of organizing the evaluation of things. My point is that monetary values should not *dominate* that evaluation, because that would be to dominate our very way of being with and managing the presence of the past generation. As I have argued throughout this chapter, the solution can never be to save everything. It is not feasible, nor is it desirable. We, the living, must *choose* what and whose data to preserve for posterity. The problem is that the capitalist economy does not allow for authentic choices, since the pursuit of any value other than profit means peril. Instead, we should aim to let as many people and perspectives as possible be part of the process. We must make this *our* choice.

* * *

Unfortunately, Roy Rosenzweig passed away in 2007 at only fifty-seven years old, right before the big breakthrough of Web 2.0. Had he been alive, he would surely have had some interesting thoughts on how to deal with the challenges ahead of us. Yet the role of the expert is not always to provide "solutions" to predefined questions. Sometimes it is just as important, if not more important, to provide the public and the scholarly community with new questions in need of answers, so as to make room for new democratic debates. This is how I see Rosenzweig's contribution, and it is what I have tried to do in this chapter. Still, my ambition has been to set out a direction for our course. Our destination, I believe, is not a place of overabundance, where we will not have to choose whose data to preserve and whose to destroy, but a place where this choice truly belongs to *us* rather than the blind mechanisms of the market. What we need is an infrastructure that allows a plurality of actors and values to be part of the process of selecting our digital remains. Now is the time to start building such systems.

5 * Living in the Post-Mortal Condition

What unites us is that, in contrast to the classic image of proletarians who have "nothing to lose but their chains," we are in danger of losing everything.

Slavoj Žižek

The ethical and political interaction between the dead and the living will always remain an open challenge, not just a case of being either with or without the dead.

Hans Ruin

In the Shoes of Max Brod

The Bohemian novelist Franz Kafka was not very famous at the time of his untimely death in 1934. Only a handful of his works, and none of the major ones, had yet been published. But the estate included several nearly finished novels and short stories, as well as diaries commenting on the works. These literary remains would never meet the public eye—at least that is what Kafka intended when instructing his friend Max Brod to burn them in the event of his death. As we all know, Brod did not comply.[1] In the years following Franz's death, Brod published three of the novels, including *The Trial*, and the diaries would later become public too. Whether or not he made the right call, ethically speaking, is up for debate. But many of us are grateful nevertheless. One may imagine that it was not an easy decision to make. Indeed, the situation put Brod in the middle of multiple conflicting moral duties. In addition to the duties to his departed friend, he had another equally compelling allegiance to the potential readers of his time, but also, and perhaps more importantly, to future readers, who, had he obeyed Kafka's request, would be refused what he saw as the literary treasure of the century. Perhaps he even felt a duty to redeem his departed friend, whose literary talents far exceeded his confidence, or to the works themselves (they simply *deserved* to be read). In any case, the custodianship of his friend's literary remains made Brod an involuntary judge between the interests of multiple stakeholders calling upon him from both the future and the past, without any clear principle by which to assess who was more righteous.

The argument of this closing chapter is that living in the post-mortal condition is to constantly find oneself in the shoes of Max Brod. By contrast to the 1930s, one does not have to write fiction or even keep a diary to leave traces of one's life behind. Insofar as you use any kind of connected device and do not actively cover up your tracks, your life becomes data whether you intend it to or not. And when you die, those data will be your digital remains, an unintentional self-portrait painted in zeros and ones. Though most people's digital remains are probably not as interesting as the diary of a master novelist like Kafka, they do nevertheless tell a story. To one's immediate family, they may be an invaluable part of the bereavement process, something to pass down to one's descendants as a memory of a beloved parent, child, or friend who died too early. Furthermore, when you add them together with those of the billions of people who have left their mark online, they become part of a pattern—a digital encyclopedia of the dead—that tells the larger story of an entire society, an invaluable resource for future generations to use to learn about their collective past. Just like Brod, a custodian of digital remains—whether an individual or an entire society—therefore has a threefold responsibility, directed both backward and forward in time: to the dead, whose wishes must be respected; to the unborn, whose access to their past is at stake; and, arguably, also to the living, who will have to sacrifice resources in order to preserve the remains.

Making sense of these responsibilities is tricky. As I argue in the following pages, it requires an ethic that takes seriously the claims of people who are temporally distant but informationally present. As a step toward such an ethic, I argue that we ought to think of ourselves as *archeopolitans*—citizens of an archive that we share with our past and its inhabitants and that we will one day hand over to our descendants. But before I go on to elaborate on the implications of this new role, let me, once and for all, and in view of the previous chapters, summarize what exactly I mean by *post-mortal* and *condition*.

The Meaning of "Post-Mortal" and "Condition"

The premise of this book is that if the dead "make civilization," any significant change in their presence, cultural or technological, is also a civilizational change. From such a standpoint, the advent of digital technology emerges as a harbinger of deep disruption. It is the herald of a new mode of being with the past and its inhabitants, a *post-mortal condition*, that replaces the "hidden death" of modernity.

By post-mortal, I mean simply a removal of the mechanisms by which the dead used to disappear from our lifeworlds. We can no longer rely on natural decay, cemeteries, or cremation furnaces to get the dead out of sight, and as such, the hiding of the dead that defined the project of modernity is coming to a definite termination. In other words, the term has nothing to do with the transhumanist notion of digital immortality, or mind uploading, whereby we "live on" though some digital surrogate brain. The dead remain as dead as they ever were, and, at least for the foreseeable future, nothing is going to change that, not even the most impressive machine learning techniques. Yet there is undoubtedly something new about the digital afterlife. The dead remain *there* for us in a way that has not been possible in pre-digital society. They remain part of our social networks, continue posting and tweeting, and, in some cases, even prevail as interactive chatbots. This is why I have compared the current situation with that of the first Paleolithic settlers. Just as they were faced with the inevitable presence of the bodies of their dead, we are now faced with the presence of the digital remains of ours. They shared their dwellings with the plaster faces of their ancestors staring back at them from the walls of their clay houses. We share our dwellings, the networked archives of the social web, with the digital faces of our ancestors, who stare, smile, and even talk back at us through the increasingly sophisticated technologies we use to animate their remains.

Even those who never left a digital footprint are subsumed by this process. As we digitize nineteenth-century photos and film, make medical and archaeological museum collections available online, and upload journals and family trees to ancestry websites, we are increasingly expanding the scope of the digital past and its population. As deep learning and other implementations of AI keep evolving, these pre-digital traces of the dead are also becoming increasingly interactive and lifelike, despite their technologically humble origins.

There is the occasional hologram performance by departed artists like Michael Jackson and Tupac Shakur. But there is also a resurgence of the past in everyday life. In 2023, the app Historical Figures, mentioned in the introduction to this book, allowed users to chat with historical figures based on information preserved about them. And two years earlier, the company MyHeritage launched an app called Deep Nostalgia, which turns old static portraits into short moving clips in which the person in the photo appears to turn their head, look around, and change their facial expression. Soon, social media was flooded with nineteenth-century faces that had suddenly been removed from their photo album slumber to become accessible to anyone anywhere on the web. Once again, they were *there* among the living. They had entered the fundamental matrix, the *house*, in which information society takes place. And this is how we should interpret the *post-mortal* part of the post-mortal condition. It is not a state of digital immortality but a mode of being wherein the past and its inhabitants remain present by default. Digital technology has abolished the mechanisms that removed the dead from our immediate proximity while at the same time recruiting the ancient dead to the realm. In short, the post-mortal condition is a new form of co-dwelling with the dead.

I describe this new co-dwelling as a *condition* because it is not given how, if at all, we as a society choose to live with the dead. As illustrated by the amazing diversity of ways by which cultures deal with their dead, there is no techno-social law that determines how the dead remain present among us. Hence, despite its obvious parallels to the first Paleolithic settlers, we must not interpret the emergence of the post-mortal condition as a retreat to some original, more natural, relationship with the dead. To once again quote Hans Ruin, "the ethical and political interaction between the dead and the living will always remain an open challenge, not just a case of being either with or without the dead."[2] The "open challenge" of how we relate to the dead, to use Ruin's words, is not neutrally manifested. It depends on the technologies by which they are mediated. But whereas digital technologies are de facto changing the rules by which we live with the dead, they do not determine the outcome. If, in the digital age, we want to continue moving the dead out of public view to maintain the "regime of life" that defined modernity, it is perfectly possible—it is just going to take a whole lot more work.[3] Yes, the advent of the post-mortal condition is inevitably the harbinger of civilizational change. Yet it is ultimately up to us, the living, to determine what that change will look like. The question is—what should it look like?

Archeopolitan Duties

In her book *All the Ghosts in the Machine*, Elaine Kasket describes the internet as a "new Elysium," a final resting place of the dead.[4] The metaphor is apt, perhaps even more apt than Kasket takes credit for. Because in Roman (and, originally, Hellenic) mythology, Elysium is not only a place of the past. It is a place *beyond* time. In Virgil's *Aeneid*, for instance, when Aeneas ventures down into the underworld, he there encounters not only his departed father Anchises, along with the other fallen heroes of the Trojan War, but also his descendants—all the way down to Romulus and Remus, the twin founders of Rome. In Elysium, time has *collapsed*. It is a place without chronology. The same is true for the post-mortal condition we find ourselves in. Our onlife life-worlds are increasingly inhabited by present and past generations alike, in a state where the past remains everywhere and everywhen, and where our dealings with the dead will have far-reaching consequences for the unborn. In the post-mortal condition, present, past, and future stakeholders all have a moral presence.

Like Aeneas in Elysium, we, the living, are the newcomers here. For as the society of the living migrates to the platforms of cyberspace, it is essentially moving into a domain that has been reserved for the dead for centuries, if not millennia: the archives. This is their territory, and we must now learn how to be part of it. Just as globalization forced us to become *cosmo*politans, citizens of the world, the post-mortal condition now requires that we learn to be *archeo*politans—citizens of the archive. What duties does this role bestow upon us? Given the analogy with globalization, perhaps the answer can be sought in what Kwame Anthony Appiah calls the ethics of cosmopolitanism. To Appiah, the ethical challenge of living in a globalized world can be described thus:

> The worldwide web of information—radio, television, telephones, the Internet—means not only that we can affect lives everywhere but that we can learn about life everywhere, too. Each person you know about and can affect is someone to whom you have responsibilities: to say this is just to affirm the very idea of morality. The challenge, then, is to make minds and hearts formed over the long millennia of living in local troops and equip them with ideas and institutions that will allow us to live together as the global tribe we have become.[5]

The problem, if I read Appiah correctly, is that modern communications have radically increased the number of people to whom we are each morally accountable. Unlike in the premodern village, closed off from the rest of the world, we now communicate and trade with people all around the globe in what Appiah calls a "global village." Space has essentially been collapsed by communication so that now we see the other, no matter how distant they are. But what are the moral implications? To Appiah, unlike other proponents of universal humanism, the answer is not a complete abandonment of local and personal allegiances. Instead, he proposes a cosmopolitan ethics that places *dialogue* at its heart. To be a true cosmopolitan, argues Appiah, is not to consistently put the interest of "humanity" above everything else but to realize that "no local loyalty can ever justify forgetting that each human being has responsibilities to every other."[6] Strangers are always human. They are entitled to moral consideration regardless of how spatially distant they may be, for, as Appiah points out, they are *informationally* present to us. Meanwhile, there is no need to let these responsibilities dominate our every action. Such an imperative may be disguised as being in the interest of everyone, but it ultimately results in the interest of no one. In short, the cosmopolitan ethics is the realization that other people around the world are *also* human.

I believe that something similar can be said about what it means to be a good archeopolitan, only that our duties extend temporally, rather than spatially. The ethical challenge is not to form ideas and institutions that allow us to live together "as a global tribe" but to live together with those who lived before us in a way that takes seriously the interests of those who will come after. For in the post-mortal condition, it is not space but *time* that has collapsed.

On the one hand, this idea calls upon us, the living, to be good descendants, or heirs. Each of us has a personal responsibility to care for the digital remains of our loved ones when they pass away, and we must do so in a way that is respectful of their wishes. Managing someone's posthumous social media presence, cleaning up the web from their unwanted traces, and preserving materials in a more permanent format on a hard drive may be part of such duties. Not reading private emails, texts, or search data of the dead may be another. As we saw in chapter 2, the digital remains of your loved ones, like their biological remains, are not your property. You are their custodian, not their owner.

As I have stressed repeatedly throughout this book, the imperative to be good heirs is also a collective responsibility, in that we need to take the ethical and political claims of the dead seriously *as a generation*. We inherit the largest archives of human behavior ever assembled in the history of our species. Making sure that that these archives are managed in a respectful manner requires institutional change, which is inevitably a collective effort. I have pointed to several examples—the #MeToo movement, the Syrian Archive's documentation of war crimes on YouTube, the Arab Spring, to name some (there are thousands more)—that tell the story of a generation that will soon be of the past but whose collective mark on the internet deserves to live on. They can do so only if we, the living, build the right institutions, the right infrastructures, and the right incentives for industry actors. To be good heirs, that is, the living need to take seriously the presence of past generations lingering on "our" servers (legally speaking, the servers belong to the industry) and recognize its political dimensions. We can only live up to such responsibilities *together*.

On the other hand, being a good archeopolitan is also to be a good ancestor.[7] It is to realize that the data you produce today will come into the hands of someone else tomorrow.

On a personal level, this means taking responsibility for your online presence beyond your lifetime. If you have not already, you should at least do the very basics. Facebook's legacy contact feature, under the heading "Memorialization settings," is one of the most visible options when choosing preferences on the website. If you are on Facebook, I suggest you stop reading, take up your phone, and fill it out. Welcome back. Most likely, many more services will ask their users to choose what will happen with their data upon the event of their death. Indeed, planning for one's digital afterlife is increasingly a moral imperative, imposed by both the industry and those next of kin who will have to "clean up your mess" unless you set things in order yourself. It is a reasonable expectation.

Just like being a good heir, the imperative to be good ancestors is also a collective one. We need to think of ourselves not only as isolated individuals, whose data will be passed down to our next of kin, but also as nodes in the network of history, as *citizens* whose data will be stewarded by those who come after us. The data trails you leave behind on the web will be an ever so tiny, but ever so important piece of the raw material out of which future generations will construct their narratives about their past. Everything we leave behind as a generation, that is, is a message for posterity saying "This happened. We think it is important that you know about it." The choice of what "this" should entail should be made consciously, at least on a structural level. For here too our responsibilities are of an institutional nature, in that we must consider what kind of institutions that should steward our collective history. What kind of materials do future generations need? How can we prevent the so-called digital dark age? And how much of our resources can we reasonably sacrifice to this end? While these are by and large institutional questions, they are, nevertheless, of an *ethical* nature. As illustrated by the environmental toll of data preservation discussed in chapter 4, it is not necessarily the case that bigger is better. Future generations may not thank us for leaving behind an endless, unstructured sea of data for them to parse through. Nor will they thank us for building massive servers at the cost of environmental sustainability (recall that the information and communication technology sector may account for as much as one-fifth of the global energy demand by 2030). Due to the scarcity of our resources, in terms of both storage capacity and ecology, we will hence have to choose what and whom to preserve, and considering the stakes involved, this choice is inevitably an ethical matter.

In sum, my proposed response to the ethical challenge of the post-mortal condition is analogous to Appiah's. We must recognize that the dead and the unborn *also* have legitimate claims when it comes to the politics of data management and protection. While their claims may not weigh as heavily as those of the living, they are nevertheless real and worthy of consideration. The dead and the unborn may not be susceptible to any "states of harm," but they are persons nevertheless, and as such they are worthy of our respect and moral consideration. As the only archeopolitans with legislative power, we ought to make sure these responsibilities are reflected in our actions.

What Is to Be Done?

The living generation has many interests in common with previous and future ones when it comes to data protection and the regulation of tech. As I have shown, the fate of digital remains is deeply entangled with the interests of living human beings. The prolongation of grief driven by an unrestrained market for digital memorials and avatars is one such example (see chapter 3). Data profiling by proxy, mining the data of a deceased relative, is another (see chapter 4). Moreover, the concentration of data records in the hands of a tiny handful of corporate actors is arguably a threat to us contemporaries, not just to future generations. As such, there are several things that we can do to live up to our archeopolitan responsibilities that would be in the interest of all of us. Without going into detail, let me point to some examples.

One thing that everyone can do is to use their consumer power to put pressure on platforms in terms of how they deal with digital remains. Since, as we have seen, markets are inherently in service only of its living consumers, the living must become allies of the unborn and the dead. In 2019, when Twitter decided to delete the inactive profiles that lingered on the network, its decision was reversed only thanks to massive protests from users.[8] In its official response, Twitter said:

> We've heard you on the impact that this would have on the accounts of the deceased. This was a miss on our part. We will not be removing any inactive accounts until we create a new way for people to memorialize accounts.

Make no mistake, Twitter would never have reversed their course had they found the net value of doing so to be negative, economically speaking. They only yielded because they realized that the accounts of the deceased were a valuable part of the user experience. Nevertheless, their response shows that voicing concerns over the management of digital remains actually does matter, at least insofar as it matters for those who hold consumer power. Likewise, one may also exercise one's democratic power (provided that one lives in a democracy) to put pressure on politicians to take our archeopolitan responsibilities seriously. Do your representatives have a plan for the long-term storage of our generation's data? What kinds of values do they believe should guide the preservation of the past? Are they ready to battle Big Tech on these matters, despite the fact that few if any of their voters will be personally affected? Just bringing the question to debate is in itself a victory. And while liberal democracy in its current format may be part of modernity's "regime of life," its members may nevertheless become allies to the dead and the unborn. [9]

What can firms do? Though I belong to those who see the term "business ethics" as an oxymoron, I contend that there are some things that businesses could do to mitigate the issues that I have discussed in this book. One of these, proposed by the English sociologist Debora Basset, among others, is to implement some kind of voluntary code of professional ethics in regard to digital remains within industries that deal with human data.[10] As I suggested in chapter 3, the International Council of Museums code of professional ethics may be an adequate model for such an arrangement. While such a code could be imposed by regulators, it could just as well be set by internal agreements within the industry or even be incorporated within the ethical policy work of individual firms. Firms could also begin to actively design their platforms with our archeopolitan duties in mind. There is already an extensive debate on so-called thanatosensitive design, that is, design that takes inheritance of digital assets seriously.[11] But this debate has largely focused on facilitating inheritance of digital assets. If we take our archeopolitan responsibilities seriously, we must also begin designing with the interests of future generations *as a collective* in mind. How can platforms be designed for long-term preservation of important historical assets? How can we facilitate future historical research, while at the same time protecting user privacy? Such matters are indeed matters of design and internet architecture.

Another obvious thing that businesses can do is share data with the public, as with Twitter's 2010 donation of its archives to the Library of Congress (see chapters 3 and 5), which was done explicitly because tweets in aggregate were seen as "a resource for future generations to understand life in the twenty-first century."[12] To be sure, there are many pitfalls here when it comes to user privacy. But for most firms, even sharing anonymized insights beyond the data shared with advertisers would be a huge step in the right direction. A prospective advertiser who opens Facebook's audience insights manager today will be provided with more detailed information about its potential audience than researchers could ever hope for. But why would Facebook's user base be more prone to share insights on their collective behavior with third-party firms than with researchers trying to understand our past? If Big Tech platforms took their social responsibility seriously, they could begin to share data. Twitter was on the right path in this regard. In 2021 it launched a product specifically for (confirmed) academic researchers that gave access to unprecedented historical data, which, I believe, was on its way to revolutionizing the way we understand our digital past.[13] Unfortunately, since Elon Musk took over the company in 2022, it has looked like access for academics will be highly limited. Moreover, for most firms, there is no financial incentive to follow suit in developing similar products. And forcing companies to share insights on their users would be a gross violation of privacy as well as the independence of private data holders.

As I proposed in a paper from 2021, a possible compromise may be the implementation of some form of "digital world heritage" label, with inspiration from UNESCO.[14] Instead of donating data to public institutions like the Library of Congress, firms could pledge to preserve the digital world heritage they hold, irrespective of its commercial value—just as states pledge to preserve the UNESCO-designated World Heritage Sites located in their territories. In return, the data holder could receive expertise from the international community on how to properly appraise and preserve the firm's archives for the benefit of future generations. Appraisal in particular would provide a valuable contribution, as most businesses are poorly equipped to assess the historical and cultural value of their data. The international community might, for example, send historians and archivists who would oversee decisions to delete data (notably, without seizing full control or ownership over them). These experts could guide both content moderation (see the example of *The Terror of War* in chapter 4) and cases where branches of a company, or particular services it provides (such as Google+), fail and are taken offline or destroyed due to lack of commercial potential. An insolvency administrator dealing with an archive with a digital world heritage label might, for example, be bound not to compromise the authenticity of the data and not to compartmentalize it. Note that the proposed label would not rely on firms pursuing any values other than their own long-term profitability. Just as a nation may benefit from having world heritage on its territory, commercial enterprises too may benefit from having the outstanding universal value of their archives recognized. Moreover, if such a treaty were signed, firms would be held to account not merely by some vague notion of morality or responsibility but by an internationally recognized contract.

Finally, perhaps the most important example of something that would be in all of our interest is to include the dead in international data protection legislation such as the EU's GDPR. Though some countries do already, to some extent, protect digital remains, this is mainly done with reference to the well-being of the deceased's living descendants. To take true responsibility would require considering the well-being of deceased data subjects in their own right. This might be through a personal but time-limited right or a right bestowed upon the next of kin. The rights of the deceased could also be shaped by extending copyright protection or could exist within what law scholar Edina Harbinja calls a "human rights–based regime," that is, as universal and inviolable rights.[15] Alternatively, these rights could be achieved by designating companies such as Facebook as "information fiduciaries," pursuant to which the companies have a duty of care to act in the best interests of users with respect to their data, including posthumously.[16] If dignity is the cardinal principle of data protection regulation, as suggested by the GDPR, then there is no reason to exclude the nonliving. Data protection is everyone's businesses.

The above proposals would be valuable improvements of our situation. Still, the diagnosis that I have made in this book is by and large of a *systemic* nature. It arises from a technical, economic, and regulatory infrastructure in service only of the living. None of the solutions suggested above addresses this shortcoming. They treat some of the symptoms, but not their cause. Moreover, it cannot be denied that there are also many ways in which the interests of different generations diverge when it comes to data management. There may be instances where the privacy of the dead conflicts with future generations' interest in their history, or where the memory of individuals from a previous generation must be sacrificed to make room for newer records. We cannot save everyone's data in a perfectly dignified format all the time. Not to speak of the growing environmental cost of data storage, discussed in the previous chapter.

This is why our situation so much resembles that of Max Brod. Brod inherited artifacts that he was told to destroy, yet he found their value to his and future generations to override that imperative. Inversely, some people inherit things they are told to preserve, while the cost of doing so eventually becomes a burden for them (I am sure many of us have that old, ugly heirloom we feel obliged to keep, though we would not exactly break down in tears if it broke or went missing . . .). The point is that in the post-mortal condition, we are constantly facing such dilemmas, both as individuals and as a society, in a way that no previous generation has. Conflicting claims reach us from both the future and the past, and our job as the first living archeopolitans is, above all, to be the arbiters of these claims.

This is a responsibility we cannot escape. If Max Brod had simply dumped Kafka's manuscripts in the hands of someone else, he would not have rid himself of responsibility. Likewise, there is no technology or system that can make our judgments for us. And this is why the marketization of our digital remains is so problematic. It reduces our choices to a mere question of profit. To the myriad of complex and nuanced questions we stand before—Whose data should be preserved for posterity? Where does one strike the line between the interests of the living versus the interests of the dead? Who should have the right to a person's digital remains?—the market has but one answer: whatever is more profitable in the long term. Sometimes this answer aligns with what we consider the correct option, and sometimes it does not.

The problem is that it does not even allow us to collectively contemplate our choices. Our goal, therefore, must be to take back control, to make this choice *ours*, as it were. Somehow, we must find a way to democratically settle upon the values that will guide the economic, technological, and regulatory systems within which the dead are mediated. Only then can we live up to our archeopolitan duties.

The nature of this project is unquestionably political, yet it does not fit neatly into any existing political narrative. Given my criticism of modernity, liberal democracy, and the capitalist market, it can certainly not be characterized as a liberal project. But perhaps a socialist one? Phrases like "take back control" and calls to abolish the dominance of the market, not to speak of my frequent references to Karl Marx, surely sound like a socialist agenda. But then again, I have categorically dismissed solutions that involve some world government seizing control of digital remains, and is not socialism part of the "regime of life" that I dismissed in chapter 1?[17] Perhaps our duty as archeopolitans is a conservative project, then? After all, my call to include past and future generations as legitimate stakeholders in our democratic communities is an almost explicit echo from Burke's notion of the social contract as an intergenerational covenant. Perhaps, but I doubt that many contemporary conservatives will join me in my fundamental critique of the capitalist market economy. Few of them would be swayed by my rhetoric of "taking back control" from industry.

So what is the road forward, then? Any concrete prescriptions for how a democratic governance of our digital past might be established, or exactly what such systems might look like, lie beyond the scope of this book. My goal has never been to propose solutions. From the outset, it has been to show how the seemingly trivial matter of dead people resurfacing on the internet is in fact deeply entangled with some of the biggest questions of our time. If I have shown that the challenges posed by the post-mortal condition cannot be solved within the covers of one single book, I consider myself successful. What I know for certain, though, is that our goal as archeopolitans must be to establish an ethical discourse in which the management of our data is not viewed exclusively as a concern of the living but one of the temporally extended, yet fragile project we know as *humanity*. Interpreting this goal will be one of the major challenges of this century, perhaps the entire millennium. I invite everyone to join in this mission. We are newcomers to the archive; let us not be its colonizers.

* * *

The fact that social media profiles linger on after a person's death may seem a trivial observation. And maybe it is. But considering that such profiles will (relatively) soon be populating the web by the billions, the consequences reach far beyond the emotional impact on the bereaved. The current generation, the first settlers of cyberspace, now finds itself in the shoes of Max Brod. We must choose how to navigate the (sometimes) conflicting interests involved. As I have tried to show in this book, what is at stake is our very relationship to our past and its inhabitants—the dead. So if it is true that the dead "make civilization," this means that our very relationship to ourselves is at stake. Indeed, as Žižek points out in the epigraph to this chapter, Marx had it wrong when he proclaimed that the proletariat have nothing to lose but their chains. As we allocate the management of our digital past to the industry, we are at risk of losing *everything*.

Epilogue

> The surest way to take possession of a place and secure it as one's own is to bury one's dead in it.
>
> **Robert Pogue Harrison**

Our story began in deep time, at the dawn of the first permanent settlements, when the dead suddenly became *present* within the immediate proximity of the living. The phenomena that I have described, analyzed, and critiqued throughout this book illustrate a similar disruption. In so doing, I am afraid the book may have painted a rather dystopian vision of a future where the past is controlled and appraised by a system that lies beyond democratic control. While still taking this vision seriously, I wish to end on a less somber note. For in the developments that I have described lie not only dangers but also an emancipatory potential.

As Harrison notes, the dead have an exceptional power to turn anonymous places into homelands, to turn a house into a home with a past, a history, and, most importantly, a forebear. Indeed, it is no coincidence that in Virgil's epic *Aeneid*, Aeneas's first priority upon reaching the Italian peninsula is to bury his fallen kin in the ground, thus turning a foreign piece of soil into a *fatherland*. Like Aeneas, we too have become settlers, only we lay our dead to rest in cyberspace rather than soil. Just as their bones once enchanted the lands upon which we build our nations and civilizations, their bytes are now buried deep in the underbelly of the online platforms that have become our new dwellings. As such, these platforms become new homes, new fatherlands, as it were, enchanted by a presence that only the dead can provide. The continuous traffic on profiles of the deceased, the public uproar every time a platform tries to change or erase them, and the strong emotional attachment observed among mourners on social media are testaments to a sense of *belonging.*

As I have observed in this book, a sense of belonging can hold great commercial potential. It provides a rare opportunity to consolidate the societal inevitability of a platform by appropriating some of the most fundamental human institutions and exploiting some of our strongest emotions: loss and kinship. Insofar as users value and care for the digital presence of the dead, they will also care for the continuation of the privately owned platforms where they remain.

Meanwhile, a sense of belonging is closely related to a sense of *entitlement.* "The surest way to take possession of a place and secure it as one's own," as Harrison notes, "is to bury one's dead in it."[1] In ancient Rome, Cicero advised against letting people bury their dead in publicly owned land, fearing it would create a sense of sacredness and thus an entitlement to the place. More recently, the tombs of ancient Hebrews in the Holy Land have frequently been used to legitimize Israel's territorial claims. As we become increasingly digital, does this mean that bereaved families in a similar way will lay claim to the platforms in which the dead are resting? Will people try to "take possession" of these sites? Will they even begin to demand access and control? It is possible. As profiles of the dead on social media begin to accumulate by the billions, so that not only individual loved ones but entire countries and generations are laid to rest there, it is plausible that the public attitude to the platforms will change. Demands for influence, indeed, even for control, may gain a new legitimacy as the dead become allies in the advocacy for democratization.

Our story ends at this fork in the road, at this dual potential. For what the future of the online dead will be is entirely up to us. Indeed, we are the new Natufians, but we also decide what that will mean.

Acknowledgments

No single person has been more important for my writing of this book than Professor Luciano Floridi, who supervised my doctoral studies at Oxford. Luciano remains a dear friend but has also had an unparalleled influence on my thinking and general understanding of what it means to do philosophy. He will always be my biggest intellectual hero. My friend and former colleague Doctor David Watson must also be mentioned. Our sometimes heated (rarely sober) debates around the pubs of Oxford have been more educational than any class I have ever taken. David has also consistently offered to read and give feedback on many of the research articles that form the empirical basis of this book, in a way that must have cost him countless hours, for which I will always be grateful. Another big thanks goes out to the many people who have read and commented on this book. Especially notable are Samuel Jonston, my wittiest and most enthusiastic critic; Johannes Rex, whose eye for the anatomy of texts never ceases to amaze me; and Professor Johan Tralau, who, with his unique knowledge and great generosity, saved me from many embarrassing mistakes and misconceptions in earlier versions of the manuscript. I should thank Maria Tengblad, who did an amazing job with the graphs in chapter 2. My gratitude also goes to the Wallenberg Foundations, who generously sponsored both my doctoral studies and, through the WASP-HS program, the first five years of my academic career.

Their devotion to academic freedom and enthusiasm for social scientific study of technology shall never be taken for granted. It goes also to the entire Department of Government at Uppsala University. I never met a kinder, more curious group of people. I am humbled to have been adopted as one of you, despite never having taken a single credit in political science. A big thank you goes out to my family, Johan, Ann, Marie, and Lisa, for always being there and believing in me. It has meant more than both you and I will probably ever understand. And finally, to Lina and Edith, who never cease to remind me that there is more to life than philosophy, and who have taught me the art of celebrating even the smallest success. I love you.

This work was funded by the Wallenberg AI, Autonomous Systems and Software Program–Humanities and Society (WASP-HS).

Notes

Introduction

Epigraph: Laqueur, *The Work of the Dead.*

1 As I cover in more detail in chapter 1, the relationship between the emergence of the first permanent settlements and the presence of the dead is a reciprocal one. Some say that settlements emerged *because* of their proximity to the dead, and not vice versa.

2 For an excellent overview of Neolithic burials, see the works of Michael Parker Pearson, especially his book *The Archaeology of Death and Burial.*

3 No single body of work has been more influential on this book than that of Harrison. If I manage to say anything of importance in the following pages, it is probably a paraphrase of him. See especially Harrison, *The Dominion of the Dead.*

4 Laqueur, *The Work of the Dead*, 81.

5 Ariès, *Western Attitudes toward Death*, 85.

6 This number is a 2016 estimate made by the research firm Gartner; see "Google Data Center FAQ," DataCenter Knowledge, March 17, 2017, https://www.datacenterknowledge.com/archives/2017/03/16/google-data-center-faq.

7 Lingel, "The Digital Remains"; Stokes, "Deletion as Second Death."

8 Kashmir Hill, "How Target Figured Out a Teen Girl Was Pregnant before Her Father Did," *Forbes*, February 16, 2012, https://www.forbes.com/sites/kashmirhill/2012/02/16/how-target-figured-out-a-teen-girl-was-pregnant-before-her-father-did/.

9 At the time of writing, Eterni.me seems to have run out of funding and is no longer online. I will discuss this further in chapter 2.

10 Öhman, Gorwa, and Floridi, "Prayer-Bots and Religious Worship on Twitter."

11 See Nick Bostrom, "Transhumanist Values," https://www.nickbostrom.com/ethics/values.html; and Steinhart, "Survival as a Digital Ghost."

12 Chapter 4 expands at length on the fragility of digital data. For a good overview of some of the issues of data preservation, see Whitt, "'Through a Glass, Darkly.'"

13 See https://www.juniperresearch.com/whitepapers/iot-the-internet-of-transformation-2020.

14 Floridi's concept is introduced in *The Onlife Manifesto*.

15 Ruin, *Being with the Dead*, 195.

16 United Nations Department of Economic and Social Affairs, "World Population Prospects."

17 Whitt, "'Through a Glass, Darkly'"; Brügger and Schroeder, eds., *The Web as History*; Graham, Milligan, and Weingart, *Exploring Big Historical Data*.

18 Rosenzweig, "Scarcity or Abundance?," 737, 753.

19 Orwell, *Nineteen Eighty-Four*, 162.

20 Rothenberg, "Ensuring the Longevity of Digital Documents."

21 Kuny, "A Digital Dark Ages?"

Chapter One

Epigraphs: Harrison, *The Dominion of the Dead*; Cicero, *Orator*.

1 In phrasing the question this way, this chapter undoubtedly owes much to Tony Walter's "Communication Media and the Dead: From the Stone Age to Facebook."

2 Laqueur, "The Deep Time of the Dead."

3 Gadamer, *Reason in the Age of Science*, 75.

4 For an elaborate exploration of animal emotion, see Bekoff, *The Emotional Lives of Animals*.

5 Harrison, *The Dominion of the Dead*, xi.

6 Harrison, 30.

7 Harrison, 72.

8 Note that not all Bedouins are nomads.

9 Mustafa and Abu Tayeh, "Comments on Bedouin Funeral Rites," 13.

10 For an elaborate analysis of the materiality not only of memory but also of the phenomenality of time, see Hägglund, *Radical Atheism*.

11 Unamuno, *Tragic Sense of Life*, 138.

12 Mumford, *The City in History*, 6.

13 As an example of just how important these landmarks were, consider that Stonehenge was probably moved because the stones represented the ancestors.

14 Parker Pearson, *The Archaeology of Death and Burial*, 160.

15 Spellman, *A Brief History of Death*, 25.

16 Parker Pearson, *The Archaeology of Death and Burial*, 164.

17 Note that there are multiple different versions of the *Epic of Gilgamesh*. The story I account for in chapter 1 is actually not the most ancient. But that detail hardly matters for the point it makes.

18 For a closer look at the connections between death and writing in ancient Egypt, see the words of Jan Assmann. In this context, I specifically recommend *Cultural Memory and Early Civilization: Writing, Remembrance, and Political Imagination*.

19 Ruin, *Being with the Dead*, 188.

20 As Heidegger notes, "Language is the house of being. In its home human beings dwell," 239

21 Parker Pearson and Ramilisonina, "Stonehenge for the Ancestors."

22 Assmann, *Cultural Memory and Early Civilization*, 75.

23 Barthes, *Camera Lucida*, 12.

24 See Burns, *Sleeping Beauty*.

25 Hallam and Hockey, *Death, Memory, and Material Culture*, 141.

26 Sconce, "Haunted Media," 28.

27 This too, I get from Harrison; see *The Dominion of the Dead*, 39.

28 Laqueur, *The Work of the Dead*, 502.

29 Laqueur, 493.

30 Troyer, *Technologies of the Human Corpse*, 28.

31 Ariès, *Western Attitudes toward Death*.

32 Ariès, 87–90.

33 Bauman, *Mortality, Immortality, and Other Life Strategies*, 137.

34 Jefferson, *Political Writings*, 593.

35 Laqueur, 493.

36 Marx, *Eighteenth Brumaire of Louis Bonaparte*.

37 The poem can be found in English translation at https://www.marxists.org/subject/art/literature/mayakovsky/1917/slap-in-face-public-taste.htm.

38 Burke, "Reflections on the Revolution in France."

39 Burke, 80.

40 Niall Ferguson, "Why the Young Should Welcome Austerity," *BBC News*, June 17, 2012, https://www.bbc.com/news/world-18456131.

41 Scruton, *The Meaning of Conservatism*.

42 This view is normally attributed to Kübler-Ross, in her classic book on grief, *On Death and Dying*.

43 United Nations Department of Economic and Social Affairs, "World Population Prospects."

44 Over the past two decades, social scientists from a wide range of disciplines have explored the effects of digital technologies on our way of relating to the dead. Understandably, the main focus has been placed on the implications for the individual internet user, who now mourns, dies, and remains dead online. Scholars of human-computer interaction like Jed Brubaker at University of Colorado Boulder and computer scientist Michel Massimi (now at Slack) have explored the implications for designers and suggested various ways of facilitating everything from shared grief and negotiating conflicting interests between stakeholders to inheritance of digital assets. Psychologists like Elaine Kasket have studied the changing patterns of grief and expressions of loss online and outlined their implications for bereavement professionals. And a long list of law scholars, most notably Edina Harbinja at Aston University, have provided both descriptive and prescriptive analyses of the legal landscape. The list goes on and on. These are much valued contributions. But as we view them in light of technological disruptions such as the emergence of the first houses, it is evident that what is at stake here is much more than merely the swiftness with which we pass on digital assets to our children, or how mourners are expressing themselves on social media. If the dead make civilization, then surely, any change to their presence is also a civilizational reconfiguration. The first Neolithic settlements fundamentally changed human societies and even our interpretation of what it means to be human. Similarly, the internet is increasingly becoming something that we dwell *inside*, and our doing so will change not only our relationship to our co-inhabitants—the dead—but, insofar as the dead *make civilization*, our relationship to all of the cross-generational project of humanity. It changes who is to be regarded a legitimate stakeholder in the question of what to do with the online dead.

45 In light of inventions like the written word and the photograph, it is clear that digital technologies are but the latest chapter in a quest as old as Gilgamesh himself: the quest of decoupling the dead person from their biological confines. Information technology, it seems, provides us prosthetic bodies made of stone, text, paper, or whatever material can best accommodate the information we want to survive. The digital disruption of our relationship to the dead is merely an incredibly effective way of preserving information, the most recent chapter in the long story of our evolving relationship to our past. Even some of the most curious social phenomena associated with digital death have ancient roots. Take, for example, the common and

well-documented conceptualization of the web as an otherworldly space where the dead can still be reached by our communicative actions. Kasket has found that roughly 77 percent of posts on deceased Facebook users' timelines directly address the deceased with phrases such as "I know you are reading this" or "Sorry I haven't been around in a while to say hi." While she stresses that this does not necessarily mean the users actually believe that the deceased can read what they write, the practice itself undeniably echoes both the ancient Egyptian interpretation of writing as a means to transcend the world of the living and also more recent technologies like the telegraph and the television.

46 Whereas the cremation furnace itself may have little relevance to the advent of digital technology, it provides a great lens through which to understand the cultural and political landscape—I referred to it as a *regime of life*—in which the current disruption of the dead is taking place. This regime is the backdrop against which we should interpret the digital disruption of our way of being with the dead. It is from this port that we depart. For in the information society, death and the dead have suddenly become everything they were not in modernity. They are emerging and will continue to emerge everywhere: in our phones, our social networks, and our servers. Their faces stare back at us from our screens like the plaster faces of Natufian skulls. Just as in the photographs in Barthes's *Camera Lucida*, they are gone, and yet they are unmistakably *there*, seemingly impossible to hide. Death, to paraphrase Parker Pearson, is no longer in opposition to life but a stage in the continuation of existence.

This break with the modern way of dealing with the dead is one of the most common observations among social scientists studying the topic, although it is not always framed explicitly as a break with modernity as such. The dead are no longer confined to hospitals and cemeteries but remain among us in our everyday living spaces. In stark contrast to the modern ideal of "getting closure" and "letting the dead go" as the ultimate destination of grief, researchers now speak of "continuing bonds." Our relationships with people are not terminated but *transformed* by death. They become "para-social," meaning that the dead person continues to be a point of reference and even the intended receiver of communicative actions. As illustrated by Kasket, among others, the dead remain part of their social networks long after the demise of their biological body.

We had better get used to seeing this type of posthumous interaction if more than 2.2 billion people are expected to pass away within the next three decades. And if internet penetration rates keep rising at their current rate, most of these dead will leave some kind of online presence behind. As I discuss in more detail in the following chapter, there is even a realistic chance that the dead will outnumber the living on Facebook within only four decades, meaning that our daily venues for communication are increasingly "para-social." To the great dismay of men like Brunetti, Thompson, and Jefferson, Mayakovsky's steamship seems to have lost its speed, and the unwanted passengers are beginning to climb back on. Just like the decision to throw them off, our way of dealing with their return is a political matter.

47 Lyotard, *The Postmodern Condition*.

48 Let me be clear that I am certainly not the first researcher to observe that the dead are present online. This is among the most common observations in the research literature. What is unique about my argument, however, is the framing of this new presence as *a civilizational change* and a process that involves all of society, rather than merely the bereaved. Death and the dead are not fringe concepts for the morbidly curious or grieving. They are fundamental categories of the social world. To read more about arguments that make observations about the presence of the dead online, see Walter et al., "Does the Internet Change How We Die and Mourn?"; Kasket, *All the Ghosts in the Machine*; Brubaker and Vertesi, "Death and the Social Network"; Graham, Gibbs, and Aceti, "Introduction to the Special Issue on the Death, Afterlife, and Immortality of Bodies and Data"; Pitsillides, Waller, and Fairfax, "Digital Death."

Chapter Two

Epigraphs: Epicurus, quoted in Diogenes and Hicks, *Lives of Eminent Philosophers*, vol. 2; Montaigne, "On Books."

1 Steinhart, "Survival as a Digital Ghost"; Carroll and Romano, *Your Digital Afterlife*; Bassett, "Ctrl + Alt + Delete"; Walter, "New Mourners, Old Mourners"; Stokes, "Deletion as Second Death."

2 The short film *Player Two* by John Wikstrom can be viewed at https://www.youtube.com/watch?v=gCtSgb-b7zg&ab.

3 Aditya Rayaprolu, "How Much Data Is Created Every Day in 2023?," *Techjury* (blog), February 27, 2023, https://techjury.net/blog/how-much-data-is-created-every-day/.

4 Al-Halbali, *The Three That Follow to the Grave*.

5 Arab Social Media Report, "Twitter in the Arab Region."

6 Bessi and Ferrara, "Social Bots Distort the 2016 U.S. Presidential Election Online Discussion."

7 I should note that at the time of our study, Du3a posted one tweet every hour. It now appears to have slowed down the pace of its posting to every second hour.

8 The transhumanists are adherents to just one of the interwoven bodies of thought that seek to achieve eternal life. Others call themselves "immortalists"; some prefer "extropianists." For a deep and wide overview of how these various movements fit together and how the dream of "mind uploading" relates to other technologies of life extension, see Farman's ethnography *On Not Dying*. This angle is, however, not within the immediate focus of this book, and so I will not elaborate in any detail on these matters.

9 Bostrom, "Transhumanist Values."

10 Bostrom.

11 Rothblatt, *Virtually Human*, 10.

12 Steinhart, "Survival as a Digital Ghost."

13 To read more about the inadequacy of anthropomorphism in artificial intelligence, see Watson, "The Rhetoric and Reality of Anthropomorphism in Artificial Intelligence."

14 This concept is introduced in Floridi, "The Informational Nature of Personal Identity," though the term is not explicitly used here.

15 Stokes, "Deletion as Second Death"; Stokes, "Temporal Asymmetry and the Self/Person Split"; Stokes, "Ghosts in the Machine."

16 Cicero, *Tusculan Disputations*, 1.43.

17 Quoted in Diogenes, *Lives of Eminent Philosophers*, vol. 2, 189.

18 This argument has been refined and developed over the millennia. Today it is known among analytical philosophers as the *termination thesis*. See Feldman, "The Termination Thesis."

19 Nagel, "Death," 78.

20 A worthy runner-up, however, which is launched with considerable detail, is Joel Feinberg's "The Rights of Animals and Unborn Generations."

21 Kant, *Groundwork of the Metaphysics of Morals, 42.*

22 Kiš, *The Encyclopedia of the Dead.*

23 Öhman and Watson, "Are the Dead Taking over Facebook?"

24 Jack Shepherd, "30 Essential Facebook Statistics You Need to Know in 2023," *The Social Shepherd* (blog), February 23, 2023, https://thesocialshepherd.com/blog/facebook-statistics-2021.

25 Öhman and Watson, "Are the Dead Taking Over Instagram?"

26 That is, the "friend"/adoptive son who betrayed Julius Caesar.

27 Montaigne, "On Books."

28 Notably, private communication is increasingly turning to encrypted channels, such as WhatsApp, and for good reason. This means that unless companies like WhatsApp are lying about not being able to unlock and mine users' chat logs, the data are useless as historical material.

29 See, for example, Roland and Bawden, "The Future of History," in which the authors interviewered historians about their thoughts on what the internet means for the future study of the past. See also Brügger and Schroeder, eds., *The Web as History*, for an enlightning overview of the emerging field of web history.

30 Rosenzweig, "Scarcity or Abundance?," 737.

31 Graham, Milligan, and Weingart, *Exploring Big Historical Data*.

32 I know not everyone is online, but bear with me for just a little longer.

33 "Social Media: What Countries Use It Most and What Are They Using?," Digital Marketing Institute, November 2, 2021, https://digitalmarketinginstitute.com/blog/social-media-what-countries-use-it-most-and-what-are-they-using.

34 Hughes makes this assertion in an interview with English Heritage.org, but I have been unsuccessful in finding the source of it. See "Why Were Women Written Out of History? An Interview with Bettany Hughes," February 29, 2016, https://www.english-heritage.org.uk/visit/inspire-me/blog/blog-posts/why-were-women-written-out-of-history-an-interview-with-bettany-hughes/.

35 Both Mayer-Schönberger, in *Delete: The Virtue of Forgetting in the Digital Age*, and Floridi, in *The Fourth Revolution: How the Infosphere Is Reshaping Human Reality*, discuss this.

36 Few have better and more accessibly illustrated the power of big data for social scientific research than Stephens-Davidowitz in *Everybody Lies: Big Data, New Data, and What the Internet Can Tell Us about Who We Really Are*.

37 Facebook is actually using machine learning to "expand our ability to identify possible suicide and self-injury content and to get timely help to people in need." Read more at Meta's "Suicide Prevention—Overview," https://about.meta.com/actions/safety/topics/wellbeing/suicideprevention.

38 Lewis et al., "Tastes, Ties, and Time."

39 Appiah, *Cosmopolitanism.*

40 Di Cosmo and Zacchiroli, "Software Heritage."

41 Meanwhile, various researchers are developing practices of what Anat Ben-David calls "counter-archiving," that is, establishing their own records from online social data available to the public. See Ben-David, "Counter-archiving Facebook."

42 Allsop, "Trash or Treasure?"

43 Rathje and Murphy, *Rubbish!*

44 Floridi, *The Onlife Manifesto.*

45 See "Inernet World Stats: Usage and Population Statistics," https://www.internetworldstats.com/.

46 Office for National Statistics, "Exploring the UK's Digital Divide."

Chapter Three

Epigraph: Marx, *Capital*, vol. 1.

1 *Black Mirror* started as a BBC Four show but has since been bought up by Netflix. The episodes of the show are freestanding (with some minor overlaps) and illustrate various hypothetical scenarios of future technologies that get out of hand. "Be Right Back" aired as the first episode of the show's second season.

2 Marcus Ursache, "The Journey to Digital Immortality," *Medium*, October 23, 2015, https://medium.com/@mariusursache/the-journey-to-digital-immortality-33fcbd79949.

3 Parmy Olson, "This AI Has Sparked a Budding Friendship with 2.5 Million People," *Forbes*, May 8, 2018, https://www.forbes.com/sites/parmyolson/2018/03/08/replika-chatbot-google-machine-learning/.

4 The entire text of US patent no. US10853717B2, can be found at https://patents.google.com/patent/US10853717B2/en.

5 Patrick May, "Mercury News Interview: Legacy Locker Founder Jeremy Toeman," *Mercury News*, April 1, 2011, https://www.mercurynews.com/2011/04/01/mercury-news-interview-legacy-locker-founder-jeremy-toeman/.

6 Mitchell et al., "Death and Grief On-Line."

7 Gustavsson, "Death and Bereavement on the Internet in Sweden and Norway."

8 For a more elaborate definition of this concept, see Öhman and Floridi, "The Political Economy of Death in the Age of Information."

9 Öhman and Floridi.

10 Brubaker and Callison-Burch, "Legacy Contact."

11 McCallig, "Facebook after Death."

12 Drew Olanoff, "You Can Take My Dad's Tweets over My Dead Body," *TechCrunch*, November 26, 2019, https://techcrunch.com/2019/11/26/you-can-take-my-dads-tweets-over-my-dead-body/.

13 Bell, Bailey, and Kennedy, "'We Do It to Keep Him Alive.'"

14 For more on the uproar that arose when Twitter announced its intent to remove deceased profiles from the network in 2020, see Billy Perigo, "Twitter Backs Down from Plan to Delete Inactive Accounts, Citing Dead Users," *Time*, November 28, 2019, https://time.com/5741218/twitter-inactive-accounts-dead-users/.

15 This cost and its consequences are discussed at length by Mayer-Schönberger in *Delete: The Virtue of Forgetting in the Digital Age.*

16 Zelizer, "Human Values and the Market."

17 Fuchs and Sevignani, "What Is Digital Labour?"

18 Kania-Lundholm, "Digital Mourning Labor."

19 Another way of framing this economic logic is through the lens on surveillance, as proposed by Harvard social psychologist Shoshana Zuboff (see Zuboff, "Big Other"). Zuboff argues that contemporary capitalism has abandoned the industrialism that once made it a desirable way of organizing the economy and that it now hinges upon the surveillance of citizens. In the case of the DAI, this would imply that digital remains are used to lure mourners into a space where they can be surveilled through the informational trails they leave behind.

20 Marx, *Capital*, 163

21 Mitchell et al., "Death and Grief On-Line."

22 Marx, *Manifesto of the Communist Party.*

23 Nissenbaum, "How Computer Systems Embody Values"; Miller et al., "Value Tensions in Design"; Friedman and Kahn, "Human Values, Ethics, and Design."

24 McLuhan, *The Medium Is the Massage.*

25 Floridi, "Infraethics," 392.

26 See ICOM, "ICOM Code of Ethics for Museums." Quotation taken from the 1986 version of the text, no longer available online.

Chapter Four

Epigraph: Orwell, *Nineteen Eighty-Four.*

1 Rosenzweig, "Scarcity or Abundance?," 737.

2 Rosenzweig, 754.

3 Rothenberg, "Ensuring the Longevity of Digital Documents."

4 Jeffrey, "A New Digital Dark Age?"; Smit, van der Hoeven, and Giaretta, "Avoiding a Digital Dark Age for Data"; Whitt, "'Through a Glass, Darkly.'"

5 Oxford law professor Viktor Mayer-Schönberger has argued that it is cheaper for companies to simply keep storing data than to appraise it, which leads to a "demise of forgetting." While there is surely something to these ideas, Mayer-Schönberger underestimates the effort it takes to maintain and keep an archive useful. The internet does indeed forget; the question is only which principles determine what falls into oblivion. See Mayer-Schönberger, *Delete*.

6 Aditya Rayaprolu, "How Much Data Is Created Every Day in 2023?," *Techjury* (blog), February 27, 2023, https://techjury.net/blog/how-much-data-is-created-every-day/.

7 See, for example, Scott Fulton III, "After Moore's Law: How Will We Know How Much Faster Computers Can Go?," Data Center Knowledge, December 20, 2020, https://www.datacenterknowledge.com/supercomputers/after-moore-s-law-how-will-we-know-how-much-faster-computers-can-go.

8 Nicola Jones, "How to Stop Data Centres from Gobbling Up the World's Electricity," *Nature* online, September 12, 2018, https://www.nature.com/articles/d41586-018-06610-y.

9 Kania-Lundholm, "Digital Mourning Labor."

10 While the GDPR explicitly only covers the rights of "natural persons," that is, not the dead, some member states of the EU have chosen to include privacy rights for the dead in their implementations of the regulation.

11 Globally speaking, Facebook users already represent only the wealthier population segments, but that does not contradict the larger point here, which is about outright *deletion* of the parts of the past that are not profitable.

12 Facebook, "FB Earnings Presentation Q4 2020."

13 As quoted in Assmann, *Cultural Memory and Early Civilization*, 56.

14 Gillespie, *Custodians of the Internet*, 1.

15 "Social-Media Platforms Are Destroying Evidence of War Crimes," *Economist*, September 24, 2020, https://www.economist.com/middle-east-and-africa/2020/09/24/social-media-platforms-are-destroying-evidence-of-war-crimes.

16 Gillespie, *Custodians of the Internet*, 1.

17 Brubaker and Callison-Burch, "Legacy Contact."

18 To read more about what has happened to the 115 million user profiles

of Myspace since its decline, see John Herrman, "What Happens When Facebook Goes the Way of Myspace?," *New York Times Magzine*, December 12, 2018, https://www.nytimes.com/2018/12/12/magazine/what-happens-when-facebook-goes-the-way-of-myspace.html.

19 It is difficult to properly assess how many users Google+ actually had. According to the company itself, the number peaked at 540 million. But as shown in an article at *Ars Technica*, creating a Google account without also creating a Google+ profile was almost impossible. The only way *not* to do so was to close the browser halfway through the account creation process. In other words, if you created your Google account (for Gmail, etc.) at some point around 2011, you are likely to be included within the reported 540 million Google+ users, possibly without knowing it. See Jon Brodkin, "Google Doubles Plus Membership with Brute-Force Signup Process," *Ars Technica*, January 22, 2012, https://arstechnica.com/gadgets/2012/01/google-doubles-plus-membership-with-brute-force-signup-process/.

20 Öhman and Aggarwal, "What If Facebook Goes Down?"

21 For a chilling overview of how data tracking works, see O'Neil, *Weapons of Math Destruction*.

22 Both Firth and Geertz are quoted on the back cover of the Stanford University Press edition of Malinowski, *A Diary in the Strict Sense of the Term*.

23 Stephens-Davidowitz, "Everybody Lies."

24 For a great take on the links between digital information and genealogy, watch Julia Creet's documentary *Data Mining the Deceased: Ancestry and the Business of Family*, 2017, https://juliacreet.vhx.tv/.

25 See Cambridge Analytica, "Administrator's Progress Report," December 12, 2018, https://beta.companieshouse.gov.uk/company/09375920/filing-history. However, consumer data (for example, in the form of customer loyalty schemes) has been valued more highly in other corporate insolvencies (see, for example, the Chapter 11 reorganization of the Caesar's Entertainment Group; JL, "Caesar's Entertainment: What Happens in Vegas Ends Up in a $1 Billion Database," Harvard Buisiness School Digital Initiative, November 22, 2015, https://digital.hbs.edu/platform-digit/submission/caesars-entertainment-what-happens-in-vegas-ends-up-in-a-1billion-database/).

26 Orwell, *Nineteen Eighty-Four*, 313.

27 Lim, *The People's Republic of Amnesia*, 96.

28 Pitsillides, Jefferies, and Conreen, "Museum of the Self and Digital Death."

29 According to a report from the World Advertising Research Centre (WARC), almost three in four users will access the internet only though mobile devices in 2025. See James McDonald, "Mobile Advertising Has Reached a Tipping Point," WARC, January 28, 2019, https://www.warc.com/newsandopinion/opinion/mobile-advertising-has-reached-a-tipping-point/2950.

30 Conservative philosophers (the real ones, not the phony people who call themselves conservatives today) are often reluctant friends of the market for this very reason. To read more about interpretations of Burke's notion of the social contract as a contract between the dead, the living, and the unborn, read Scruton, *The Meaning of Conservatism.*

31 Smith Rumsey, "When We Are No More," 143.

Chapter Five

Epigraphs: Žižek, "How to Begin from the Beginning"; Ruin, *Being with the Dead.*

1 In the name of posthumous fairness, I should add some nuance to this story by mentioning that Brod was always clear with Kafka that he refused to burn the manuscripts. Kafka chose him to steward his estate anyway, so it clearly could not have meant the world for him to have the manuscripts destroyed.

2 Ruin, *Being with the Dead*, 195.

3 Laqueur, 493.

4 Kasket, *All the Ghosts in the Machine*.

5 Appiah, *Cosmopolitanism,* xiii.

6 Appiah, xvi.

7 For more on how to be a good ancestor, see Krznaric, *The Good Ancestor.*.

8 Billy Perigo, "Twitter Backs Down from Plan to Delete Inactive Accounts, Citing Dead Users," *Time*, November 28, 2019, https://time.com/5741218/twitter-inactive-accounts-dead-users/.

9 Laqueur, 493.

10 Basset, *The Creation and Inheritance of Digital Afterlives: You Only Live Twice. Springer*

11 Ellis Gray, "Remains in the Network"; Massimi, "Thanatosensitively Designed Technologies for Bereavement Support"; Markova, "Digital Dying in Personal Information Managementt."

12 Raymond, "The Library and Twitter."

13 Read more about how Twitter used to help researchers in Adam Tor-

res, "Enabling the Future of Academic Research with the Twitter API," Twitter Developer Platform, January 26, 2021, https://developer.twitter.com/en/blog/product-news/2021/enabling-the-future-of-academic-research-with-the-twitter-api.

14 Öhman, "The Case for a Digital World Heritage Label."

15 Harbinja, "Does the EU Data Protection Regime Protect Post-Mortem Privacy?," 20; see also Sandvik, "Digital Dead Body Management."

16 See Balkin, "Information Fiduciaries and the First Amendment."

17 Laqueur, 493.

Epilogue

Epigraph: Harrison, *The Dominion of the Dead.*

1 Harrison, *The Dominion of the Dead.*

Bibliography

Al-Halbali, Ibn Rajab. *The Three That Follow to the Grave*. Birmingham, UK: Dar as-Sunnah, 2016.

Allsop, Laura. "Trash or Treasure? Sifting through Ancient Rubbish for Archaeological Gold." CNN, October 4, 2011. https://edition.cnn.com/2011/10/04/world/europe/archaeology-ancient-trash/index.html.

Appiah, Kwame Anthony. *Cosmopolitanism: Ethics in a World of Strangers*. London: Penguin, 2008.

Arab Social Media Report. "Civil Movements: The Impact of Facebook and Twitter." http://arabsocialmediareport.com/Twitter/LineChart.aspx. [Original site currently offline; archive available at https://www.yumpu.com/en/document/view/29618788/arab-social-media-report-dubai-school-of-government.]

Ariès, Philippe. *Western Attitudes toward Death: From the Middle Ages to the Present*. Translated by Patricia M. Ranum. Baltimore: Johns Hopkins University Press, 1974.

Assmann, Jan. *Cultural Memory and Early Civilization: Writing, Remembrance, and Political Imagination*. Cambridge, UK: Cambridge University Press, 2011.

Balkin, Jack M. "Information Fiduciaries and the First Amendment." *UC Davis Law Review* 49, no. 4 (2016): 1183–234.

Barthes, Roland. *Camera Lucida: Reflections on Photography*. New York: Hill and Wang, 1981.

Bassett, Debra J. *The Creation and Inheritance of Digital Afterlives: You Only Live Twice.* Cham, Switzerland: Palgrave Macmillan, 2022

Bassett, Debra J. "Ctrl + Alt + Delete : The Changing Landscape of the Uncanny Valley and the Fear of Second Loss." *Current Psychology* 40 (2021): 813–21.

Bauman, Zygmunt. *Mortality, Immortality, and Other Life Strategies*. Cambridge, UK: Polity Press, 1992.

Bekoff, Marc. *The Emotional Lives of Animals: A Leading Scientist Explores Animal Joy, Sorrow, and Empathy—and Why They Matter*. Novato, CA: New World Library, 2007.

Bell, Jo, Louis Bailey, and David Kennedy. "'We Do It to Keep Him Alive': Bereaved Individuals' Experiences of Online Suicide Memorials and Continuing Bonds." *Mortality* 20, no. 4 (2015): 375–89.

Ben-David, Anat. "Counter-archiving Facebook." *European Journal of Communication* 35, no. 3 (2020): 249–64.

Bessi, Alessandro, and Emilio Ferrara. "Social Bots Distort the 2016 U.S. Presidential Election Online Discussion." *First Monday* 21, no. 11 (2016). https://doi.org/10.5210/fm.v21i11.7090.

Brubaker, Jed R., and Vanessa Callison-Burch. "Legacy Contact: Designing and Implementing Post-Mortem Stewardship at Facebook." In *CHI '16: Proceedings of the 2016 CHI Conference on Human Factors in Computing Systems*, ed. Jofish Kaye and Allison Druin, 2908-19. New York: Association of Computing Machinery, 2016.

Brubaker, Jed R., and Janet Vertesi. "Death and the Social Network." Presented at the CHI 2010 Workshop *HCI at the End of Life: Understanding Death, Dying, and the Digital*, Atlanta, March 2010. https://dl.acm.org/doi/10.1145/1753846.1754178.

Brügger, Niels, and Ralph Schroeder, eds. *The Web as History: Using Web Archives to Understand the Past and the Present*. London: UCL Press, 2017. https://discovery.ucl.ac.uk/id/eprint/1542998/1/The-Web-as-History.pdf.

Burke, Edmund. "Reflections on the Revolution in France." Lawrence, KS: Neeland Media, 2004. First published London, 1790.

Burns, Stanley B. *Sleeping Beauty: Memorial Photography in America*. Altadena, CA: Twelvetrees Press, 1990.

Carroll, Evan, and John Romano. *Your Digital Afterlife: When Facebook, Flickr and Twitter Are Your Estate, What's Your Legacy?* Berkeley, CA: New Riders, 2011.

Cicero, Marcus Tullius. *Orator*, in *Brutus. Orator*. Translated by H. M. Hubbell. Cambridge, MA: Harvard University Press, 1939.

Cicero, Marcus Tullius. *Tusculan Disputations*. Translated by C. D. Yonge. New York: Harper & Brothers, 1877. Retrieved from Project Gutenberg, 2005. https://www.gutenberg.org/files/14988/14988-h/14988-h.htm.

Di Cosmo, Roberto, and Stefano Zacchiroli. "Software Heritage: Why and How to Preserve Software Source Code." Presented at *iPRES 2017, 14th International Conference on Digital Preservation*, Kyoto, September 2017. http://www-archive.cseas.kyoto-u.ac.jp/ipres2017.jp/wp-content/uploads/19Roberto-Di-Cosmo.pdf.

Diogenes, Laertius. *Lives of Eminent Philosophers*, vol. 2. Translated by Robert Drew Hicks. Cambridge, MA: Harvard University Press, 1925.

Ellis Gray, Selena. "Remains in the Network: Reconsidering Thanatosensitive Design in Loss." PhD diss., Lancaster University, 2015. https://doi.org/10.13140/RG.2.1.4817.2249.

Facebook. "FB Earnings Presentation Q4 2020," 2020. https://s21.q4cdn.com/399680738/files/doc_financials/2020/q4/FB-Earnings-Presentation-Q4-2020.pdf.

Farman, Abou. *On Not Dying*. Minneapolis: University of Minnesota Press, 2020.

Feinberg, Joel. "The Rights of Animals and Unborn Generations." In *Philosophy and Environmental Crisis*, edited by William T. Blackstone, 43–68. Athens: University of Georgia Press, 1974.

Feldman, Fred. "The Termination Thesis." *Midwest Studies in Philosophy* 24, no. 1 (2000): 98–115.

Floridi, Luciano. *The Fourth Revolution: How the Infosphere Is Reshaping Human Reality*. Oxford: Oxford University Press, 2014.

Floridi, Luciano. "The Informational Nature of Personal Identity." *Minds and Machines* 21, no. 4 (2011): 549–66.

Floridi, Luciano. "Infraethics—On the Conditions of Possibility of Morality." *Philosophy and Technology* 30, no. 4 (2017): 391–94.

Floridi, Luciano, ed. *The Onlife Manifesto: Being Human in a Hyperconnected Era*. Cham, Switzerland: Springer, 2015. https://library.oapen.org/bitstream/handle/20.500.12657/28025/1001971.pdf.

Friedman, Batya, and Peter H. Kahn Jr. "Human Values, Ethics, and Design." In *The Human-Computer Interaction Handbook: Fundamentals, Evolving Technologies and Emerging Applications*, edited by Julie A. Jacko and Andrew Sears, 1177–201. Mahwah, NJ: Erlbaum, 2002.

Fuchs, Christian, and Sebastian Sevignani. "What Is Digital Labour? What Is Digital Work? What's Their Difference? And Why Do These Questions Matter for Understanding Social Media?" *TripleC* 11, no. 2 (2013): 237–93.

Gadamer, Hans-Georg. *Reason in the Age of Science*. Cambridge, MA: MIT Press, 1983.

Gillespie, Tarleton. *Custodians of the Internet: Platforms, Content Moderation, and the Hidden Decisions That Shape Social Media*. New Haven, CT: Yale University Press, 2018.

Graham, Connor, Martin Gibbs, and Lanfranco Aceti. "Introduction to the Special Issue on the Death, Afterlife, and Immortality of Bodies and Data." *Information Society* 29, no. 3 (2013): 133–41.

Graham, Shawn, Ian Milligan, and Scott Weingart. *Exploring Big Historical Data: The Historian's Macroscope*. London: Imperial College Press, 2016.

Gustavsson, Anders. "Death and Bereavement on the Internet in Sweden and Norway." *Folklore (Estonia)* 53, (2013): 99–116. https://doi.org/10.7592/FEJF2013.53.gustavsson.

Hägglund, Martin. *Radical Atheism: Derrida and the Time of Life*. Palo Alto, CA: Stanford University Press, 2008.

Hallam, Elizabeth, and Jenny Hockey. *Death, Memory, and Material Culture*. Oxford: Berg.

Harbinja, Edina. "Does the EU Data Protection Regime Protect Post-Mortem Privacy and What Could Be the Potential Alternatives?" *SCRIPTed* 10, no. 1 (2013): 19–38.

Harrison, Robert Pogue. *The Dominion of the Dead*. Chicago: University of Chicago Press, 2010.

Heidegger, M. "Letter on Humanism." In *Pathmarks*, edited by William McNeill, 239–76. Cambridge: Cambridge University Press. 1998. Originally published 1946.

ICOM. "ICOM Code of Ethics for Museums." Paris: ICOM, 2017. https://icom.museum/wp-content/uploads/2018/07/ICOM-code-En-web.pdf.

Jefferson, Thomas. *Political Writings*. Edited by Joyce Appleby and Terence Ball. Cambridge, UK: Cambridge University Press, 1999.

Jeffrey, Stuart. "A New Digital Dark Age? Collaborative Web Tools, Social Media and Long-Term Preservation." *World Archaeology* 44, no. 4 (2012): 553–70.

Kania-Lundholm, Magdalena. "Digital Mourning Labor: Corporate Use of Dead Celebrities on Social Media." In *Death Matters: Cultural Sociology of Mortal Life*, edited by Tora Holmberg, Annika Jonsson, and Fredrik Palm, 177–97. Cham, Switzerland: Springer, 2019.

Kant, Immanuel. *Groundwork of the Metaphysics of Morals*. Cambridge: Cambridge University Press, 1998.

Kasket, Elaine. *All the Ghosts in the Machine: How the Digital Age Is Transforming Death in the 21st Century*. Boston: Little, Brown, 2019.

Kiš, Danilos. *The Encyclopedia of the Dead*. London: Penguin, 2015.

Krznaric, Roman. *The Good Ancestor: How to Think Long Term in a Short-Term World*. London: W. H. Allen, 2021.

Kübler-Ross, Elisabeth. *On Death and Dying*. London: Routledge, 2009.

Kuny, Terry. "A Digital Dark Ages? Challenges in the Preservation of Electronic Information." *International Preservation News* 17, no. May (1998): 8–13.

Laqueur, Thomas W. "The Deep Time of the Dead." *Social Research* 78, no. 3 (2011): 799–820.

Laqueur, Thomas W. *The Work of the Dead: A Cultural History of Mortal Remains*. Princeton, NJ: Princeton University Press, 2016.

Lewis, Kevin, Jason Kaufman, Marco Gonzalez, Andreas Wimmer, and Nicholas Christakis. "Tastes, Ties, and Time: A New Social Network Dataset Using Facebook.com." *Social Networks* 30, no. 4 (2008): 330–42.

Lim, Louisa. *The People's Republic of Amnesia: Tiananmen Revisited*. Cary, NC: Oxford University Press, 2014.

Lingel, Jessa. "The Digital Remains: Social Media and Practices of Online Grief." *Information Society* 29, no. 3 (May 2013): 190–95.

Lyotard, Jean-François. *The Postmodern Condition: A Report on Knowledge*. Minneapolis: University of Minnesota Press, 2010.

Malinowski, Bronislaw. *A Diary in the Strict Sense of the Term*. Stanford, CA: Stanford University Press, 1989.

Markova, Katerina. "Digital Dying in Personal Information Management: Towards Thanatosensitive Information Management." Masters thesis, University of Porto, 2011. https://www.researchgate.net/publication/304946288_Digital_Dying_in_Personal_Information_Management_Towards_Thanatosensitive_Information_Management.

Marx, Karl. *Capital: A Critique of Political Economy*, vol. 1. Marxists Internet Archive, 1999. https://www.marxists.org/archive/marx/works/1867-c1/. First English edition published 1887 by Progress Publishers (Moscow).

Marx, Karl. *The Eighteenth Brumaire of Louis Bonaparte*. Marxists Internet Archive, 1999. https://www.marxists.org/archive/marx/works/1852/18th-brumaire/. First English edition published 1937 by Progress Publishers (Moscow).

Marx, Karl. *Manifesto of the Communist Party*. Marxists Internet Archive, 2000. https://www.marxists.org/archive/marx/works/1848/communist-manifesto/ch01.htm. First English edition published 1888 by Progress Publishers (Moscow).

Massimi, Michael. "Thanatosensitively Designed Technologies for Bereavement Support." PhD diss., University of Toronto, 2012. https://tspace.library.utoronto.ca/bitstream/1807/32766/3/Massimi_Michael_201206_PhD_thesis.pdf.

Mayer-Schönberger, Viktor. *Delete: The Virtue of Forgetting in the Digital Age*. Princeton, NJ: Princeton University Press, 2009.

McCallig, Damien. "Facebook after Death: An Evolving Policy in a Social Network." *International Journal of Law and Information Technology* 22, no. 2 (2014), 107–40.

McLuhan, Marshall. *The Medium Is the Massage*. London: Penguin, 2008.

Miller, Jessica K., Batya Friedman, Gavin Jancke, and Brian Gill. "Value

Tensions in Design: The Value Sensitive Design, Development, and Appropriation of a Corporation's Groupware System." In *Proceedings of the 2007 International ACM Conference on Supporting Group Work (GROUP '07)*, edited by Tom Gross and Kori Inkpen, 281–90. New York: Association for Computing Machinery, 2007.

Mitchell, Lisa M., Peter H. Stephenson, Susan Cadell, and Mary Ellen Macdonald. "Death and Grief On-Line: Virtual Memorialization and Changing Concepts of Childhood Death and Parental Bereavement on the Internet." *Health Sociology Review* 21, no. 4 (2012): 413–31.

Montaigne, Michel de. "On Books." In *Essays*, edited by William Carew Hazlitt and translated by Charles Cotton. London: Reeves and Turner, 1877. https://hyperessays.net/essays/on-books/.

Mumford, Lewis. *The City in History: Its Origins, Its Transformation, and Its Prospects*. London: Penguin, 1991.

Mustafa, Mairna H., and Sultan N. Abu Tayeh. "Comments on Bedouin Funeral Rites in the Writings of Western Travelers and Explorers from the Late 19th and Early 20th Centuries." *Mediterranean Archaeology and Archaeometry* 14, no. 1 (2014): 51–63.

Nagel, Thomas. "Death." *Noûs* 4, no. 1 (1970): 73–80.

Nissenbaum, Helen. "How Computer Systems Embody Values." *Computer* 34, no. 3 (2001): 119–20.

Office for National Statistics (UK). "Exploring the UK's Digital Divide." 2019. https://www.ons.gov.uk/peoplepopulationandcommunity/householdcharacteristics/homeinternetandsocialmediausage/articles/exploringtheuksdigitaldivide/2019-03-04.

Öhman, Carl. "The Case for a Digital World Heritage Label." *Information & Culture* 57, no. 1 (2022): 82–95.

Öhman, Carl, and Nikita Aggarwal. "What If Facebook Goes Down? Ethical and Legal Considerations for the Demise of Big Tech." *Internet Policy Review* 9, no. 3 (2020): 1–21.

Öhman, Carl, and Luciano Floridi. "The Political Economy of Death in the Age of Information: A Critical Approach to the Digital Afterlife Industry." *Minds and Machines*, 27, no. 4 (2017): 639–62.

Öhman, Carl, Robert Gorwa, and Luciano Floridi. "Prayer-Bots and Religious Worship on Twitter: A Call for a Wider Research Agenda." *Minds and Machines* 29, no. 2 (2019): 331–38.

Öhman, Carl, and David Watson. "Are the Dead Taking Over Facebook? A Big Data Approach to the Future of Death Online." *Big Data and Society* 6, no. 1 (2019): 1–13.

Öhman, Carl, and David Watson. "Are the Dead Taking Over Instagram?

A Follow-up to Öhman & Watson (2019)." In *The 2020 Yearbook of the Digital Ethics Lab*, edited by Josh Cowls and Jessica Morley, 5–21. Cham, Switzerland: Springer, 2021.

O'Neil, Cathy. *Weapons of Math Destruction: How Big Data Increases Inequality and Threatens Democracy*. New York: Broadway Books, 2017.

Orwell, George. *Nineteen Eighty-Four*. London: Secker and Warburg, 1949.

Parker Pearson, Michael. *The Archaeology of Death and Burial*. Stroud, UK: Sutton, 1999.

Parker Pearson, Michael, and Ramilisonina. "Stonehenge for the Ancestors: The Stones Pass on the Message." *Antiquity* 72, no. 276 (1998): 308–26.

Pitsillides, Stacey, Janis Jefferies, and Martin Conreen. "Museum of the Self and Digital Death: An Emerging Curatorial Dilemma for Digital Heritage." In *Heritage and Social Media: Understanding Heritage in a Participatory Culture*, edited by Elisa Giaccardi, 56–68. London: Routledge, 2012.

Pitsillides, Stacey, Mike Waller, and Duncan Fairfax. "Digital Death: What Role Does Digital Information Play in the Way We Are (Re)Membered?" In *Digital Identity and Social Media*, edited by Steven Warburton and Stylianos Hatzipanagos, 75–90. Hershey, PA: IGI, 2012.

Rathje, William L., and Cullen. Murphy. *Rubbish!: The Archaeology of Garbage*. Tucson: University of Arizona Press, 2003.

Raymond, Matt. "The Library and Twitter: An FAQ." *Timeless: Stories from the Library of Congress* (blog), April 28, 2010. https://blogs.loc.gov/loc/2010/04/the-library-and-twitter-an-faq/.

Roland, Lena, and David Bawden. "The Future of History: Investigating the Preservation of Information in the Digital Age." *Library & Information History* 28, no. 3 (2012): 220–36.

Rosenzweig, Roy. "Scarcity or Abundance? Preserving the Past in a Digital Era." *American Historical Review* 108, no. 3 (2003): 735–62.

Rothblatt, Martine Aliana. *Virtually Human: The Promise—and the Peril—of Digital Immortality*. New York: Picador, 2015.

Rothenberg, Jeff. "Ensuring the Longevity of Digital Documents." *Scientific American* 272, no. 1 (1995): 42–47.

Ruin, Hans. *Being with the Dead: Burial, Ancestral Politics, and the Roots of Historical Consciousness*. Stanford, CA: Stanford University Press, 2019.

Sandvik, Kristin Bergtora. "Digital Dead Body Management (DDBM): Time to Think It Through." *Journal of Human Rights Practice* 12, no. 2 (2020): 428–43.

Sconce, Jeffrey. "Haunted Media: Electronic Presence from Telegraphy to Television." Durham, NC: Duke University Press, 2000.

Scruton, Roger. *The Meaning of Conservatism*. South Bend, IN: St. Augustine Press, 2014.

Smit, Eefke, Jeffrey van der Hoeven, and David Giaretta. "Avoiding a Digital Dark Age for Data: Why Publishers Should Care about Digital Preservation." *Learned Publishing* 24, no. 1 (2011): 35–49.

Smith Rumsey, Abby. "When We Are No More: How Digital Memory Is Shaping Our Future." New York: Bloomsbury USA, 2016.

Spellman, W. M. *A Brief History of Death*. London: Reaktion, 2015.

Steinhart, Eric. "Survival as a Digital Ghost." *Minds and Machines* 17, no. 3 (2007): 261–71.

Stephens-Davidowitz, Seth. *Everybody Lies: Big Data, New Data, and What the Internet Can Tell Us about Who We Really Are*. New York: Harper Collins, 2017.

Stokes, Patrick. "Deletion as Second Death: The Moral Status of Digital Remains." *Ethics and Information Technology* 17, no. 4 (2015): 237–48.

Stokes, Patrick. "Ghosts in the Machine: Do the Dead Live On in Facebook?" *Philosophy and Technology* 25, no. 3 (2012): 363–79.

Stokes, Patrick. "Temporal Asymmetry and the Self/Person Split." *Journal of Value Inquiry* 51, no. 2 (2017): 203–19.

Troyer, John. *Technologies of the Human Corpse*. Cambridge, MA: MIT Press, 2021.

Unamuno, Miguel de. *The Tragic Sense of Life in Men and Nations*. Translated by Anthony Kerrigan. Princeton, NJ: Princeton University Press, 1978.

United Nations Department of Economic and Social Affairs. "World Population Prospects: The 2017 Revision." New York: United Nations, 2017. https://population.un.org/wpp/publications/files/wpp2017_keyfindings.pdf.

Walter, Tony. "Communication Media and the Dead: From the Stone Age to Facebook." *Mortality: Promoting the Interdisciplinary Study of Death and Dying* 20, no. 3 (2015): 215–32.

Walter, Tony. "New Mourners, Old Mourners: Online Memorial Culture as a Chapter in the History of Mourning." *New Review of Hypermedia and Multimedia* 21, no. 1–2 (2015): 10–24.

Walter, Tony, Rachid Hourizi, Wendy Moncur, and Stacey Pitsillides. "Does the Internet Change How We Die and Mourn? Overview and Analysis." *Omega: Journal of Death and Dying* 64, no. 4 (2011): 275–302.

Watson, David. "The Rhetoric and Reality of Anthropomorphism in Artificial Intelligence." *Minds and Machines* 29, no. 3 (2019): 417–40.

Whitt, Richard S. "'Through a Glass, Darkly': Technical, Policy, and Financial Actions to Avert the Coming Digital Dark Ages." *Santa Clara High Technology Law Journal* 33, no. 2 (2017): article 1. http://digitalcommons.law.scu.edu/chtlj/vol33/iss2/1.

Zelizer, Viviana. "Human Values and the Market: The Case of Life Insurance and Death in 19th-Century America." *American Journal of Sociology* 84, no. 3 (1978): 591–610.

Žižek, Slavoj. "How to Begin from the Beginning." *New Left Review* 57 (May/June 2009). https://newleftreview.org/issues/ii57.

Zuboff, Shoshana. "Big Other: Surveillance Capitalism and the Prospects of an Information Civilization." *Journal of Information Technology* 30, no. 1 (2015): 75–89.

Index

Page numbers in italics refer to figures.